ANIMAL
LEGACIES

REBECCA HALL GRUYTER
#1 INTERNATIONAL BEST SELLING AUTHOR

Published 2019
Printed in the United States of America

Print ISBN: 978-1-7328885-4-8

Publisher Information:
RHG Media Productions
25495 Southwick Drive #103
Hayward, CA 94544

www.YourPurposeDrivenPractice.com

Acknowledgements

When writing an anthology, it takes many voices to be willing to join together to bring forth the book in a powerful and united way. It has been such an honor and privilege to work with this amazing group of heartfelt authors as they lean in and trust us with these personal and powerful chapters. I want to thank these amazing experts for entrusting us to bring forth and share their powerful animal legacies.

I want to thank my husband for always cheering me on and encouraging me to SHINE! I thank God for giving me opportunities, opening doors, and bringing together the right people for this powerful project. Thank you Mr. Patches, Shelby, Sherman, Nina Tina, Mocha Bean, Darla, and Alfie. I thank my parents for their love and support and my grandmothers for planting the legacy seeds to always choose to Bloom Where You Are Planted, Step Forward, and SHINE!

Contents

FOREWORD
BY BETTYANNE GREEN

Fluffy, Butterscotch, Cookie, Bear, Madeline of Newtown, Figaro, Cleo, Cinnamon, Mitsurugi, Killarney, Kira, Tekka. These are all the names of precious animals who have touched my heart and enriched my life in some way. Most are pets we adopted into our family (or, rather, they adopted us). I might also add the animal friends from television, books, and movies who kept me company throughout my childhood, like Lassie, Black Beauty, Old Yeller, Fury, Lady and Tramp, and every single one of the 101 Dalmations.

As I write this, my grandpup Tekka, a black and white border collie, sits by my side, every so often giving me a gentle nuzzle to invite me to scratch her ears. She is a loving, scary-smart dog who has these subtle, polite ways of communicating which we now know so well, including one I discovered moments ago, which makes me giggle every time: Tekka lets us know she is bored and wants attention, not by barking or leaping on our laps...nope! Instead, she takes just one small piece of Kleenex or something similar out of the wastebasket and sets it on the floor nearby. She does not rip it up, she does not tip the basket over or pull out a bunch of trash – just one small item to let us know she has something to say!

I am sure you have similar stories of special animals in your life. I would even bet that you have told stories about your pet around the dinner table, shown your friends adorable photos from your phone, and reminisced about pets long gone but still remembered lovingly and with a tear in your eye. Perhaps you have had an unforgettable "chance" encounter with an animal that changed you forever. Maybe you know you have a spirit animal who guides and protects you.

> "Until one has loved an animal a part of one's soul
> remains unawakened." ~ Anatole France

As you read the stories in this beautiful book, I suspect you too will call up names and memories of precious animals who have had a profound influence on your life in some way. You might discover from these amazing authors how your soul may have awakened in wondrous ways that you never thought of before, because of the imprint of an animal upon your life.

This is the magic of this book – to remind us that the connection between humans and animals runs very deep. When we are open to what animals can teach us, our lives are enriched and our souls are awakened.

Within these pages are stories of animals who have shown their unfailing love, reliable friendship, unconditional acceptance, courage and tenacity. Stories of animals who help "pull us more deeply into the spirit of the natural world," and pets who are "divine mirrors for our souls." A story of imaginary animal friends who kept a child company during lonely times, through grief and loss. Memories shared of a loving pet who stood by protectively to keep a little girl safe in an unsafe household. And confessions of a self-proclaimed Cat Lady who unapologetically owns her title.

We get to learn about rescuing unwanted dogs and volunteering at shelters; how to tune in to get heart-to-heart with your pet; the interesting lives of crows; and how we can discern through our pets' behavior the messages they are meant to teach us. We even get to hear a dog's side of the story!

I am very grateful to these open-hearted authors who, each in their unique way, celebrate and honor animals who have left powerful imprints (pun intended) on their lives, brought them so much joy and taught them profound life lessons. We are the lucky recipients of their beautiful experiences and the legacies these animals have left on their lives ...and now on our own.

Welcome to the magical world of Animal Legacies. I hope you will become as enchanted and touched as I have been in reading this wonderful book!

Bettyanne Green

Bettyanne Green is a Content Marketing Strategist and Concierge Copywriter who helps heart-centered business owners give voice to the purpose behind their products, through marketing messaging that matters – to the marketplace, to their bottom line, and toward a world that works for everyone.

With more than 35 years of experience in marketing communications, writing and graphic design, Bettyanne has worked in almost every aspect of the craft, for clients ranging from *The New York Times*, the League of Women Voters, international development magazines, The Cleveland Orchestra, political campaigns and civic change efforts, to entrepreneurs and small business owners.

Bettyanne's unique business model is based on a concierge relationship with her clients so they can deep-dive together to craft, strategize, and consistently deliver a results-driven message while honoring and lifting up the truth her clients yearn to tell. If you are curious about how your business marketing could be more impactful and exciting, please reach out to Bettyanne at **Bettyanne@Heart2HeartMarketing.com**.

Content Marketing Strategist | Concierge Copywriter
Heart 2 Heart Marketing
http://heart2heartmarketing.com/about/
https://www.linkedin.com/in/bettyannegreen/
https://www.facebook.com/Bettyanne.Green.Copywriter/
https://twitter.com/mixedbag1

SECTION 1:

Caring Canine Connections

LOVE MAKES ALL THINGS POSSIBLE
BY SUZANNE THIBAULT

Love makes all things possible. This is what my childhood dog Wiggles taught me. Her unconditional love saved my life.

Wiggles was a small, white, curly-haired mutt with a fluffy tail. She was my best friend as a child growing up in a highly dysfunctional family. Her loving animal guidance showed me that love makes all things possible, because her love was bigger than my fear.

Let me take you back in time. I grew up in a household where I was not wanted or loved. I felt like an outcast in my own family, and was so alone. I knew I did not fit in by the way my parents treated me. All I ever wanted as a child was to be loved. But I was not without love–I knew my dog Wiggles loved me. She was always by my side, making me laugh as we played together. She would cuddle next to me on the couch and lick my hand. Her love was kind and so important to me. **Growing up in a household without love, I found comfort in knowing that Wiggles loved me.**

At age eight my parents left me home alone while they went on vacation to Tahiti for two weeks. This was very traumatic for me. It was not like the movie "Home Alone" where 8-year-old Keven goes grocery shopping and orders pizza. I fell straight down the rabbit hole into traumatic fear, feeling terrified, shocked, and ashamed. My small body shook with fear, so much so that I could not handle it, and I screamed out in pain. This is when I first heard Wiggles speak to me. She said, "Don't be afraid, you are not alone. I am here with you and I love you!" Somehow hearing her loving words lifted me up and out of that deep pit of fear. I looked at her in amazement and I gave her hug. Wiggles' love was bigger than my fear.

I do not believe I would have survived that trauma without Wiggles by my side. Being abandoned and rejected by my parents broke my heart into a million little pieces, but it also allowed me to experience, for the first time, the true unconditional love of an animal which healed my heart. **Today, through the unfailing love of animals, I am a professional animal communicator and emotional healer, supporting animal lovers to effectively communicate with their pets and shine the light onto emotional pain for heart healing to make peace with the past.**

Animals that grace our lives are angels in disguise. Maybe you do not have a pet now, but at some point in your life I imagine that you have connected with an animal. **The human/animal bond runs deep; it is a spiritual bond so strong that it can never be broken.** Pets are the only living beings on Earth that love you more than you love yourself. **Animals are our guiding lights that shine brightly when we feel lost. All you have to do is focus on their love and it will change your life forever.**

Pets help us to reach our truest potential. They awaken and expand human awareness, love, and compassion. They open your heart to seeing and living life in a different way. Your pet is helping you gain a better understanding of yourself and the world around you by helping you tap into a part of your heart that you might not be able to reach yourself. **As you glimpse life through the eyes of your beloved pet, you come to understand who you really are.**

Your connection with your pet goes much deeper than you might realize. Your pet knows how to read your energy and understands how you are feeling. That understanding helps them to support your life by showing you, through behavior, how to look at your life differently. In this way your pet is your teacher, healer, and supporter of your life. When you notice your pet's loving guidance you can change your perspective.

Animals as Teachers

Animals are our teachers, as they provide loving animal guidance for our personal growth. The problem is, most people are not aware of this gift of love. Animals have their own behavioral issues that mirror how you are feeling inside. This shows you what you are holding inside that might need to change. For example, let's say your normally mellow, cuddly cat becomes easily agitated and standoffish. You might think there is something wrong with her. Instead of wondering what's wrong with her, you can ask yourself, "What is my cat trying to tell me?" Look at your current life–are you easily agitated and standoffish with people, pushing them away? When you notice what is going on in your own life and choose to change, then your cat's behavior will change too, and she will return to her normal cuddly self. This is hands and paws learning and growing together with animals as our teachers.

Animal Guidance

The simplest form of animal guidance comes through the animal's behavior that reflects to us what we hold inside. **Because animals are highly adept at sensing your energy, they then act out through behavior as a form of communication.** Animals will show you aspects of yourself that need support and nurturing. Becoming aware of animal guidance helps you see what needs to change in your own life.

If you have a pet then you are already understanding many of their behaviors and body language. When you walk in the door, your dog jumps for joy to see you, even if you were only gone a few minutes! They are expressing their joy-filled love for who you are. Your cat will come and lay next to you when you are feeling sick to provide comfort and companionship. Those types of behaviors are easy for you to see and interpret. Pets celebrate life with you, through all the ups and downs, with their powerful love leading the way. Animal guidance is easy and simple to see and appreciate once you are aware of it.

It is about respecting each other enough to learn from each other.

Pets will exhibit boundary, behavior, or health issues to grab your attention. When you worry about your pet's health and wellbeing, they have gotten your attention! This is when you can start getting curious about your pet's guidance.

How to Notice Animal Guidance

If your animal is showing you unusual behaviors then observe the animal's actions, think about what you can learn from it, and take action for yourself. It's about getting curious! While some animal behavior stems from the animal's own emotional pain, a great majority of their behaviors serve as guidance for human personal growth.

If your dog chews up your favorite pair of shoes, they are not being spiteful. Your pet's behavior is not saying, "Oh she makes me so mad! I'm going to chew up her shoe and show her." Animals are not spiteful and they do not judge you. You might react to your ruined shoes by thinking, "What a jerk!" or "What is wrong with you?" Your frustration is a signal to you to begin looking inside yourself for answers. Are you angry about anything going on in your life? Is anyone in your life being unkind or malicious towards you? The animal's behavior is teaching you something about yourself.

This is how your pet is fully supporting your life. They help you to grow personally by showing you what is inside that no longer serves you, so you can heal it. It is a beautiful gift of love and support.

You can begin noticing animal guidance by:

- Using your awareness to notice your animal's subtle behaviors.
- Asking yourself if the behavior applies to you or them.
- Asking yourself, "How might this behavior apply to my life?"
- If you see the connection to you, take their message to heart and choose to change.

Here are a few examples to help you understand how to start noticing animal guidance:

Example 1: Your dog is outside. You call him to come in and he stands there staring at you, not moving. You ask again and he just stands there. You get frustrated and impatient. Your dog is not being a jerk. **Ask yourself, "What is my dog trying to tell me? Do I need to have more patience? Am I stalling on something or not moving forward in some way?"** Once you realize something about yourself, you can take action to heal and bring positive change to your life.

Example 2: You have been working for hours on your computer. Your cat saunters into the room and sits directly on your keyboard so you have to stop typing. **Ask yourself, "What is my cat trying to tell me? Let's see, do I need to take a break? Do I need to stop what I'm working on and move onto something else? Or do I need to slow down and have a cup of tea?"** It is a simple, beautiful process of self-discovery.

Example 3: Your dog has been licking her feet so much that a sore has developed. You are concerned about her health and the vet thinks the excessive licking is stress related. **Ask, "What is my dog trying to show me? Am I dealing with anxiety or depression? Am I feeling any stress about anything?"** That is animal guidance in action.

The key here is to take the animal's behavior and see how it applies to your own life. By observing our animals we can improve our own lives. If you can identify the issue within your life, you can work on changing it, and then your pet's behavior will improve.

You will see animal guidance naturally and be able to look inside and understand if it applies to your life. You mentally scan through what is currently going on in your life and see if any animal guidance fits. Remember, your pet senses something inside of you that you are not yet aware of and you are working to bring that up and out of yourself.

You know your pet well. Noticing their messages will be easy for you. Essentially, you become an investigator. Some behavior or health issues can benefit from animal communication as it might be your pet's personal issue, and some are a reflection for your own life. You investigate by having the courage to look at your life and see if something is showing up for change, then taking action.

Animal guidance is a gift of love for your personal and spiritual growth. Be courageous and receive this gift from your pets. They are small and large angels assisting you in life, offering a healing partnership for both of you. Open your heart to the possibilities of their unconditional love in action. May you discover and embrace who you really are through your pet's loving guidance.

The love of a dog saved my life, teaching me that love makes all things possible. What if your pet could do the same for you? The legacy that my dog Wiggles has imprinted upon my heart is that animals are our partners in life. It is through their unconditional love that we can heal and grow on a personal level to heights we can only imagine. Allow the animal(s) in your life to inspire you to heal your life through animal guidance, as hands and paws are better together!

Suzanne Thibault

Suzanne inspires and challenges women to deepen their relationship with animals and spirit for their self-care. She takes a stand for her client's personal and spiritual growth, supporting both women and animals to embrace their life potential through the foundation of emotional heart healing that dramatically improves their life. Through divine healing, Suzanne shines the light on emotional pain that leads to heart healing as they make peace with the past.

Her core message, that *Love Makes All Things Possible*, was born from her childhood dog Wiggles saving her life as a young child in a highly dysfunctional family. She learned then about the animal/human bond of unconditional love that is so strong it transforms your life, and now shares this wisdom with animal lovers everywhere. Look for her book, *Animal Wisdom Tales, Messages of Love from Pets and Wild Animals*, on Amazon.

As the podcast host of Spiritual Straight Talk, Suzanne inspires with a prophetic voice to support your relationship with spirit. As the founder of Suzanne Thibault Academy, she imparts to others the spiritual teachings of animal communication and divine inner healing through the Holy Spirit.

To Learn More:

Email: **soul-safari@outlook.com**
Business Phone: (916) 426-8068
Website: **https://www.suzannethibault.net/**
Training Website: **https://suzanne-thibault-academy.thinkific.com/**
Facebook: **https://www.facebook.com/suzanne.thibault.549**
Instagram: **https://www.instagram.com/suzanne.thibault_/**

Spiritual Straight Talk Podcast:
https://www.suzannethibault.net/category/podcast/

MY FIRST NEPHEW
BY NEELAM WADHWANI

Pom Frite's Story

Have you ever found yourself sitting in a room, surrounded by a noisy crowd, and feeling completely and totally alone? Well, that is where I found myself one day, late in April of 2007. I had been "surrendered" by my mistress the day before, and I was upset! I mean, how could I NOT be?! **This was the second time that I had lost my person, and I was only two and a half years old!**

What difference had that specialized training made? It hadn't stopped Master Benji from leaving me (well...actually, he had died, so maybe I had come out the winner on that one). And what about the way I had bounced back after breaking my leg over and over again? Mistress Hilda STILL had the nerve to surrender me!

Well...to heck with them! I am here now, and THIS person seems nice enough. But I will be damned if I ever let myself get attached to anyone... ever again! (So there!)

Moneeka's Story

I was lying in my bed in the middle of the day and crying. I had just suffered another miscarriage. This was my twelfth! I was heartbroken, once again. I was also exhausted. I couldn't do this anymore; I didn't have it in me. So I cried some more knowing that I had come to the decision to stop trying to have a baby.

The weeks and months that followed were a blur to me. I had descended into a state of despair. The blooms of spring couldn't inspire me. The summer sun couldn't lift my spirits.Then, on the evening of my fifteenth wedding anniversary, my husband gave me the surprise of my life! He announced that "we" were getting a puppy! I couldn't believe it! I thought he was joking. But when I realized that he wasn't, a flicker of hope seeped back into my weary heart.

Over the next few days, my husband and I pondered breeds, size, age, and furriness. After much deliberation, we decided on a Pomeranian–it was small enough to keep in our condo and furry enough to snuggle with. We were excited that we made our decision. Now what?

Well, let's see... where do we find such a creature? And that is how we began our search. We started at the shelters, but we didn't connect with any of the dogs there.

So we branched out and looked elsewhere. We turned our attention to little-dog rescue organizations, and we found many! But most of them didn't have Pomeranians. Now what?

Well, if shelters and little-dog rescues didn't seem to have what we were looking for, then who would? We looked into rescues that cater specifically to Pomeranians. But, we found that they were few and far between. There were a few, my husband reminded me. I kept my complaints about the "far between" to myself.

Our journey took us from San Jose, to San Francisco, and up through the Sonoma Valley. Soon we were scaling expansive landscapes of rolling hills and sprawling vineyards. Nestled within this glorious scenery was where we finally found what we were looking for.

In Sebastopol, CA, around forty minutes outside of Santa Rosa, stood a houseful of rescued Pomeranians. Their "person" was a

20-something-year-old young woman, who, admittedly, was struggling to make ends meet. But her obvious commitment and sheer determination to rescue, rehabilitate, and re-home these divine little animals, impressed us.

So one fine morning, on a Saturday in early October, we started out for this "haven in the hills". After winding our way through places my father used to refer to as "God's country" for nearly two hours, we finally turned into the gravelly driveway that would lead to our final destination: Misty's Pomeranian Retreat. I was so excited! I could hardly wait.

As I looked on, my mind began to churn. What kinds of dogs would I meet? What kinds of personalities would they have? Would I like them? Would they like me? What if...?! We had come so far, and I wasn't about to turn back! With a deep breath, I clasped my hands together and brought them to my chin. Then, I waited... itching to get a glimpse of the furry little creatures I had wanted to connect with so badly.

Pom Frite's Story

I felt them before I saw them. Then, a blue Rav4 rumbled up the drive and came to a stop right behind the pen I was sitting in. That is when I first laid eyes on them. They were both fussing about as they peered through the windshield. The moment they stepped out of their vehicle, **I could feel their anxiety. It was a mixture of anticipation and pain that resonated with me instantly! That's when I knew, right then and there, that these were the people I was meant to settle down with! They were "my" people!** As they walked around the corner towards the front door, I raced through the house to meet them. My "here and now" person noticed, and looked up. Moments later, the doorbell rang.

Moneeka's Story

Misty, the lady I had spoken with on the phone, answered the door. She was taller than I had expected, and she had long, strawberry-blonde hair. She introduced herself and invited us to come in. The moment we stepped inside, I noticed the tiny little dog sitting attentively to one side, barely able to contain himself.

"Hmm...that's unusual", said Misty as she looked on. "He's never done that before!"

The dog she was referring to was a tiny Pomeranian whom I had seen sitting stoically alone in the pen outside as we drove up. I found him curious then, and I found him curious now, too. I stooped down to say hello, but the little dog was having none of it. Instead, he trotted right past me and into the path of my husband.

My husband wasn't sure what to make of that. Surprised, and a little amused, even, he knelt down and pet him. "Hello, little guy. Well, aren't you friendly?"

I watched them, and wondered what had just happened. But a few minutes later, the little dog trotted over and sat right in front of me. Then he scooted forward and placed his head beneath my partially-outstretched hand. Delighted, I obliged him with a gentle caress. I was reveling in the softness of his fur, so I missed the look of astonishment that came over Misty's face. But my husband caught it, and he enquired.

"I have never seen him behave this way", Misty said quietly, looking intensely at the little dog. "I guess he really likes you guys." But she didn't seem particularly pleased with this idea.

"That's a good thing, right?" My bewilderment was obvious.

"Well, I don't know," Misty said, sounding more bewildered than I was. Then she glanced at her watch and perked up. "Oh, no! I have to go! I will be late for work." *What? We drove all this way, and now she has to run?* Misty saw the disappointment on our faces. She sheepishly informed us that her work had called her in at the last minute, because they were short-handed. "But we can meet up, again, in a few hours, if you want?"

Well, that was a surprise. First, she was in a hurry despite the impression I had been given on the phone that she had cleared her schedule and would be available to us for as long as it took. Second, she wanted us to stick around so we could meet up with her later. I looked at my husband, and he looked at me. And then we both looked at Misty and said, in unison "Sure".

We took one last look at the fluffy, little Pomeranian, who had returned to sitting attentively to one side, and then left.

You and I must make a pact. We must bring SALVATION back!
(Mariah Carey, I'll Be There)

Pom Frite's Story

Huh? What? You're leaving? No...don't leave! You CAN'T leave! We were meant to be together... wait! FINE! Be that way! I'll just wait right here in this very spot until you come to your senses and return for me.

Moneeka's Story

As we drove away, my heart grew heavy. Who was that little dog anyways? Why did he single me out? Did he know how sad and empty I felt? Could he feel my isolation?

We pulled up in front of Whole Foods Market, and parked. Then we just sat there. Neither one of us seemed ready to get out of the car and find something to eat.

"That was a friendly little dog." My husband just put it out there.

What did he mean by that? I wasn't sure, so I said, "Yeah! No kidding!" Three and a half hours later, we were back on Misty's doorstep.

She answered the door on the second knock. Anxiety was written all over her. But when she recognized us, she began to relax. As she greeted us and ushered us inside, It was almost as if she was relieved to see us. But she still didn't seem particularly happy to see us.

As soon as Misty closed the door behind us, we saw the fluffy little Pomeranian whom I had been so preoccupied with all day. He was still sitting in the exact same spot that he had been in when we had left earlier in the day. When he saw us, he came to life! He sprung up on all fours, yapped a greeting to us, spun in circles a couple times, and then sat down again, barely able to control his enthusiasm. It was as if he was saying, *Welcome Back! I knew you'd return!* But how did he know? Did he feel the same way we had?

Misty followed our gaze, and shook her head with that same look of astonishment on her face, that she had had before. "He hasn't moved from that spot since you left! And now he's barking and dancing around like never before!" Me and my husband both looked up. That caught our attention.

Misty went on to tell us that this particular little dog had already suffered two great losses in his young life, and that she was inclined to hold on to him to give him a chance to heal. And even then, she wasn't sure she wanted to re-home him, because she didn't want him to suffer anymore!

But she hadn't anticipated the way he had reacted to us. This both surprised and worried her, and she shared as much with us.

Well, Misty wasn't the only one. I was astounded! Two people had abandoned this adorable little fur ball? How could that be? This little dog's story had resonated so loudly in me, that I couldn't hear myself think! I looked at my husband and he looked at me. Moments later, he broke our gaze and turned to say something to Misty. But I didn't hear it. I was focused on the precious little creature sitting in front of me.

"Moneeka? Moneeeeeeeka?" My husband snapped his fingers to get my attention. "What do you think?"

I looked over at him. "Huh? What did you say?"

"He's taken a liking to us, and, frankly, I've taken a liking to him too. What do you think?"

"I think..." I turned back to the little dog. "I like him, too..." I said, almost wistfully. A little while later, I noticed that my husband was preparing to leave. Where was he going? I had decided that I wasn't leaving without this precious little boy!

"Moneeka?" he called out to me, again. No! I wasn't ready to leave! I looked over at him with mutiny in my eyes. He shook his head and chuckled softly. "Don't worry, Sweetheart," he said. "I know how you feel. And I'm with you." My husband smiled. "I've arranged it with Misty already. We are taking him home."

Pom Frite's Story

Wait...did he just say what I think he said? Really? REALLY!

Moneeka's Story

His name was Rory. And he was sitting on my lap in the front seat of our car as my husband steered it out of the driveway and onto the main road. I couldn't believe it! We had finally found the "one", and we were bringing him home!

Over the next couple of days, my husband and I decided that the name Rory didn't suit such a large personality wrapped up in such a tiny little package. So we renamed him Pom Frite, after the delectable little potato strips we so enjoyed munching on during our stay in Europe. He was such a delectable little creature!

****

It took Pom Frite about three years to settle in to his new home. He kept expecting Moneeka and her husband to get rid of him every time he made a mistake (like when he had an accident on the carpet or when he broke his leg when he jumped off the sofa). But when his expectations weren't met, time and time again, he began to relax. And a new hope blossomed, one of having found his forever home!

Moneeka's life changed the moment she brought the fluffy little Pomeranian home! Little Pom Frite was truly a part of her life now, and she was ecstatic! Not only had she found the cutest little dog in the whole world, but she had also found another wounded soul in need of healing, and she was up to the task.

Neelam Wadhwani

Neelam Wadhwani is a talented writer who writes on cultural topics related to Hinduism, in niche magazines and blogs, upon request. She is a creative type who has used her formal education to springboard her way into new cultural experiences, both at home and abroad.

Neelam holds a Master's degree in cross-cultural education, with credentials in teaching. She has taught English as a Second Language to students in Japan, Switzerland, and throughout the United States. She even worked for a time at a Montessori preschool, where she applied the new techniques that she had learned to complete her daily responsibilities.

These days, you'll find her splitting her time between assisting her elderly parents, doting over her 1st nephew, studying financial securities, and writing a book inspired by her own spiritual journey about Hinduism.

https://www.facebook.com/neelam.wadhwani.96
(916) 695-5512

GRAND SCHEME FROM THE HEAVENS
BY KATHLEEN E. SIMS

I looked across the large room filled with adoptable dogs, looking for my two grandsons. There they were, grinning from ear to ear, sitting on the floor with a large black dog lying next to them. They all looked happy. I motioned for them to come over to the middle of the room where I was, in front of a pen of adorable fluffy puppies. I said, "Look. How about one of these cute puppies to take home?" They looked at them for a couple of minutes, then disappeared, returning to the black dog on the other side of the room. I was not drawn to go over to the dog they seemed to have claimed as their own. He was full-grown, fairly large, and had short, black hair with a white chest.

I looked again at the puppies in front of me. They were so animated, soft and cute. I did notice that they had big feet. I had to admit to myself they did look like Saint Bernard puppies, which concerned me about their size when full-grown and our household's ability to accommodate such a large dog.

One of the volunteers at the Pet Adoption Agency walked over and asked me if I was thinking of adopting one of the puppies. I replied, "Yes; I think they are adorable."

She started asking me questions, like if I had a job. When I told her I do work, she responded with, "You can't adopt these puppies because they need to be confined to a place in your home and raised by a family in which someone in the household is home most of the time. It takes about two years to train them into well-mannered adult dogs. It does not sound like your home is equipped to take proper care of a puppy."

I was stunned by the reality she was describing. It brought me back to a time years ago when we did have a dog we raised from a puppy and had for her entire life. I remembered her chewing our shoes and the furniture when she was a puppy, and how much work it was. I felt kind of nauseous just remembering it.

I was surprised at the lack of interest from my grandsons in the cute puppies. However, I do not give up easily. I called them over one more time, just in case I could change their minds. They came back over just to humor me and the same scene repeated itself. They looked on in disinterest and then returned to the big black dog. I was disappointed, yet partly relieved at the same time.

I decided I needed to find out what was so appealing about the big black dog the boys were attached to. I walked all the way across the large room passing many different breeds and sizes of potential family pets. There they were, sitting on the floor next to this very quiet and calm adult dog laying next to them. I asked the dog's foster dad what he thought about this dog. He said, "His name is Odie. He is very well behaved and trained. We think he is about five years old, half Labrador and half Greyhound." The foster dad decided it was time to take him out on the leash for a break. As they stood up and started walking out, I saw how Odie stayed perfectly by the foster dad's knee, heeling and walking in slow motion to not pass him. He was so well-mannered and regal. That was it for me; he was "finished product" of effective dog training. Right then and there I decided this dog was actually "the one", much to my surprise. "Okay boys. We'll take Odie home and try him out to see if he fits into our family."

The first night Odie wanted to sleep on the bed with Josh. Later that evening I went into Josh's room to say goodnight, and Odie was on the edge of his bed. Much to my surprise, he growled at me. He appeared to be protecting Josh. I went out of the room confused, wondering if we made a bad choice.

By the end of the next week, Odie was following me around like he was my shadow. Wherever I went he would lie down by my feet, waiting quietly for whatever was next. Even though he was large he was so calm, quiet, and well behaved; he seemed invisible.

In the second week of dog ownership, we got a call from the Pet Adoption Agency, asking us if we had cats. I said, "Yes, we have two cats." They said in their database they realized Odie was the only dog they had that was listed as a cat predator. They asked me if he had harmed my cats yet. I said, "No, but he seems to chase them. However, the cats hiss and scare him away." The woman on the phone demanded that I return the dog or I would come home one day to a tragedy finding one of my cats dead. That was a horrifying thought. By this time I was very attached to Odie and resisted her demand. She called for three weeks in a row, to check if my cats were still alive. They were and they continued to stand up for themselves, so Odie left them alone.

My sweet husband of forty years, Jim, had no idea when we married in high school that I would be an ongoing animal rescue person, creating an animal menagerie–cats, dogs, and horses. He loved the animals, but he was not a collector like I was.

I took Odie with me to the mountain where I kept my horses so he could be the trailblazer on my horse rides several times a week, taking his long, Greyhound strides on the trails all over the mountain. Odie was so happy.

One morning Jim, Josh, and Odie came in the house after doing their morning paper route together. Josh went to his room to get ready for school. Jim passed me in the hall and enfolded me in a long, sweet hug. "Everyone is yearning for this kind of love and connection, Kathleen," he said to me. "And most people don't even know it exists."

Then Jim went to the kitchen to cook breakfast for Josh and I. I went back into the bedroom when suddenly I heard a very loud noise that sounded like something heavy had dropped on the floor in the kitchen. I hollered to Jim, "What fell?" No answer. I hollered again, "Jim what happened?" There was no answer. I got up and ran to the kitchen and there he was laying on the floor on his back, unconscious. I asked Josh to call 911 and watch for the fire truck as I rushed to give mouth-to-mouth resuscitation. I was able to bring Jim back to consciousness several times, but I lost him again each time. The firemen arrived and connected him to a machine to jump start his heart again. I could not believe my eyes; there laid my husband of forty years at the young age of sixty, an athlete at that, and it appeared he had a heart attack. His last words of a special love expressed to me rang in head, like a message from heaven.

The ambulance took him to the hospital and he was announced dead on arrival. How could this happen? We had never talked about this situation as a possibility. I thought we would live a long life together into our eighties or nineties. By the end of that day I went to bed in shock and exhaustion.

That night I was sitting up in bed, leaning back against the headboard writing a list of things I had to take care of the next day. Odie was laying in Jim's empty spot in the bed. He was sound asleep, facing the foot of the bed with the length of his body against my leg, when all of a sudden an intense energy came into my head making my teeth chatter uncontrollably. Then I felt the energy move into my chest, down the torso of my body and into Odie's body.

I could see the energy moving quickly throughout his body, causing it to shake like my teeth. Then the energy moved up into Odie's head. He was sound asleep and all of a sudden he started making a sound like a human crying; it did not sound like a dog crying or a dog dreaming. It sounded like a person crying, wailing and sobbing. It lasted about seven or eight minutes and then there was complete silence. Odie did not wake up the entire time. This energy ritual repeated itself for 3 nights in a row. I was shocked, yet awestruck. It seemed we had several visitations from Jim's spirit expressing his shock and deep sorrow over his own passing.

In preparation to have guests over after Jim's celebration of life, my house was filled with people helping out. Friends and family were working very hard to complete the patio that Jim had been building but had not completed. My house is on a court with only three houses and both of my side gates were open for delivering bricks and cement.

I was standing in the driveway with Odie in front of Jim's truck when my phone rang and it was Denise, one of my daughters, who was thirty miles away. She said she was on her way to my house, and that there was a butterfly on her windshield that would not leave. She stopped the car to pull over and brush him off. The butterfly kept coming back, landing again on her windshield. As I was talking to her and facing Jim's truck, I looked down and all over the front of the grill there were hundreds of white butterflies. Odie gently walked over to look more closely at them.

I described to Denise the butterflies I was seeing all over her dad's truck, at the same time Denise was standing by her car with one butterfly not taking flight off of the windshield. Suddenly the white butterflies on Jim's truck started swarming and swirling together as Odie acutely focused on them. They started lifting in a swarm higher and higher up into the sky, as Odie ran in circles like a dog chasing his tail, ecstatically jumping up and down, until we could not see the butterflies anymore.

He then ran down the side of the house, around the back, up the other side of the house, and out into the court running in a circle as fast as he could and back into the first gate, again running in a circle around the house and back out to the street. He did this three times like he was on a race track and then he landed on the driveway panting and resting, yet still excited. I was still on the phone with Denise describing what was happening. Right then the butterfly lifted off of her windshield and flew away. It seemed like Odie had assisted Jim's spirit and soul's transition back into the light. In his ecstasy for Jim's soul's release he demonstrated what was happening, and helped me understand this surreal and magical process. Odie was my miracle companion, like an angel expressing Jim's grief and loss of life, along with miraculously accompanying his soul's return back into the light.

Looking back over all these events, of which at the time looked like stand alone situations, I see the divine plan at work in a myriad of ways, and the grand scheme from the heavens.

Can you look back over events in your life and recognize the greater purpose and gifts bestowed upon you from the heavens?

I was very blessed to have Odie's companionship for three more years helping me through my grief and loss. When I think back to that first fateful day when I was in such conflict about bringing Odie home, obviously something greater than myself was at work, with many gifts from the heavens, guiding my grandsons to encourage me to make the right choice by bringing home our sweet animal guide and angel.

THE LEGACY OF A STORM CLEARING
TO UNCONDITIONAL LOVE
BY LORRAINE GIORDANO

I stood alone in the dark, staring out my living room window into the ominous, murky, sewage-filled water inching closer to where I stood. I lived on the first story of an apartment building few blocks from the New York city skyline. The water lapping against the foundation of the building taunted me as though it were coming closer to swallow me and my sanity. My worst-case scenario plan-if the rising water reached my home-was to climb five stories to the roof and wait to be rescued. My hands shook slightly as I took small sips of room-temperature water from the glass I held. My apartment was three stair steps up from the others on the first floor. Some of my neighbors' apartments down the hall had been infiltrated hours earlier. Undercurrents of dread, worry, and feeling stuck swirled inside me. Would another storm surge of water caused by Hurricane Sandy bring devastation to my sanctuary that stood below sea level?

Mother Nature aggressively made herself known with the storm's arrival on October 29, 2012. This Category 2 storm had downgraded to a post-tropical cyclone by the time it hit the Northeast Although it hadn't brought a lot of rain to Hoboken, where I lived, the dramatic surge of ocean water had engulfed the area with flooding never experienced during my time there. As I stared out my window for hours, in disbelief,

I acknowledged that Hurricane Sandy had triggered a Category 5 storm inside my head. In many healing traditions, the element of water is tied to emotions, and this hurricane bubbled up hidden feelings that, until that point, I'd done a good job distracting myself from.

What would this storm be like if I were married and/or had children and was with them now? Would I be happier or not? It was great that I'd saved my uterus from a hysterectomy and reclaimed my health in 2008, but had I missed an opportunity after reclaiming my uterus, to possibly have a baby even when my gynecologist told me I wouldn't be able to? Early in my healing journey, a fertility specialist refused to treat me because she thought the threat of cancer was too high. Instead of IVF treatments, she recommended oncologists. My what-if scenarios bubbled up. Those tough moments created some cracks in my foundation. Who was I if I hadn't given birth or didn't have a child? By saving my uterus (an effort I'd termed Operation Save Uterus), I'd discovered a deep well of power I hadn't recognized until then. During the storm, I wondered who I was without a child even though I found this deep well of power. Would I ever feel free from how society equates a woman's identity with birthing and motherhood?

Pacing in the dark without the normal distractions of light, ambient noise, the TV, or phone, my thoughts blared as loud as a 1980s boom box. The two firemen paddling a canoe down what had recently been my street, and was now a river, didn't distract me from the inner surge of intense, raw, uncomfortable feelings. I wanted to run away but was held hostage by sewage water, fumes, and the weight of the past.

I asked God to help me out of this trapped place that felt scary, isolated, and dark. God answered. It didn't take long. The gentle voice said, *move away from the window and sit down.* I perched on the end of my chaise lounge, focused on the sound of my breath, and closed my eyes. A few minutes later, another message came in the same calm, peaceful voice: *the work you'll do will soothe whatever loss you feel about not giving birth to a baby. Mothering comes in different forms. Breathe. Remember this message. It's time for you to move.* Then the sweet whisper said, *get the dog that you've wanted to get for years.* The last two messages surprised me. I thought the voice was going to tell me to get an expensive renter's flood insurance policy.

Two months after the storm, still feeling lucky that I'd been spared from any flooding in my place, I honored the message about moving.

Finding a new place was easy. The hard part was all the objections in my head to stay in a post flood, mold-filled building: my apartment was cheap and had so much space; too much time was needed to clean out all the clutter I'd amassed over the years; I was healing from sewage PTSD from the storm; and so on. Luckily, the desire to get a dog kept me motivated and focused to move forward.

Sometimes disastrous moments shift the earth under our feet. We are forced to find a new place to root ourselves and start again. I'm fortunate that I didn't lose the contents of my home like so many others did during Hurricane Sandy. The storm's violent wind hit me in a profound way that unsettled me enough to replant my life on higher ground with the help of my little Louie-a nine-pound Maltipoo (part Maltese/part Poodle breed). I'd listened to those messages.

Louie and I met when I answered an ad from a Maltipoo breeder a few towns away. The Maltipoo mix was a homage to my family's dog Sheppy, a poodle, and Honeybee, a Maltese that my family had when I was growing up and into my twenties. Sheppy and Honeybee were instrumental peace agents in our house.

Although Louie and I hit it off immediately, each of his brothers and sisters were adorable and clamored for attention when I went to select a dog from the litter. We all played in the breeder's back courtyard. I shared a lot of giggles, and they happily wagged their tails and jumped around each other, and me. My bag was on the ground as I played with the puppies. When I wasn't playing with Louie, he'd climb onto the top of my bag as if to say, "You're taking me home!" I originally planned to call my new dog Sharpie because of my love for Sharpie markers. But this tiny pup, with apricot tipped ears, and bright eyes staring back at me resembled an older Italian man. I knew he wasn't a Sharpie because he reminded me of my Grandpa Louie-my dad's dad, who had suddenly passed away from a heart attack when I was eleven. My favorite memories of my grandpa involved playing catch with him. I suspected my little Louie and I would have fun with future games of catch.

"Fur baby" is a common term used these days. I'm not a fan of "fur baby" to describe my relationship. Louie is just Louie—my dog. With that said, he's more to me than a best friend or wing man. He is family—my family. He's an energetic bundle of unconditional love that licks, barks, cuddles, and is a strong communicator. His influence has touched me deeper than I ever imagined.

During the past seven years, my little Louie has emerged as a valuable teacher and roommate. Relationships with the fellas might come and go—but Louie is a keeper. Here are six powerful lessons I've learned from receiving my sweet, smart friend into my life.

1. Invite Yourself In

Oddly enough, while on daily walks, Louie likes to invite himself into neighbors' homes all the time. He uses his charm and persistence to wiggle himself into their houses to say hi to their animals-including cats-and anyone else inside. His confident approach has made me ask myself how I can invite myself into the life I desire to create? Can I explore new opportunities and invite myself in, rather than wait to be invited?

When I first got Louie, it was around the same time I left corporate America and started my energy healing practice, Inspired To Health. Starting a business requires commitment, faith, and determination. **Louie's example of inviting himself to take part in new adventures rather than being invited has helped me reach out and explore different contacts and opportunities to expand not only my business, but also my relationship with others.** The amazing friends I've made, thanks to Louie's friendly approach, have rippled outward, creating new lifelong friendships that I treasure.

2. Communication Comes in Many Forms

Louie sets a clear example of using his voice by barking if he's hungry, wants to play, needs more water, sees or hears another dog outside, or has concerns about thunder and fireworks. He doesn't hold back from expressing himself when he wants attention. He's guest starred in many of my *Womb Happy Hour* radio show episodes, assisted with sharing kisses and hugs during many client's sessions, and gets a lot of shout outs on social media posts. **He uses is voice with purpose.**

For most of my life I didn't use my voice to speak my truth. In my own healing process and that of my clients, it's common to notice patterns of repressed expression. It's easy to feel unsafe or avoid how we feel and steer clear of talking about it. Louie's bark is a regular reminder about how important it is for me to express my voice and share my truth without apologies, and be willing to express the boundaries that work for me. That expression ripples out in the messages I share with my clients, and it flows out in their personal experiences.

3. Just because You Don't See it Doesn't Mean it's Not There

Louie's sense of smell is a lot more potent than mine. According to Psychology Today, dogs can have up to 225 million scent receptors in their nose, compared to the 5 million scent receptors in humans. (**https://www.psychologytoday.com/us/blog/canine-corner/201101/do-some-dog-breeds-have-better-noses-and-scent-discrimination-others**)

He sniffs out treats, bully sticks, and balls, that I can't see, and barks until I get it for him. There are many times I don't believe that there's something he wants beyond a closed door or under the couch. Sometimes I find it annoying, because he uses his voice loudly to confirm that there's something for him that's not in plain sight. His expression says, "I know it's there. If you change your point of view and tune in differently, you're going to see it's there too." A lot of times seeing it requires moving a piece of furniture and getting on the floor to change my perspective, and lo and behold, I do see what he's trying to get. This kind of sense is like the energy work I do as alternative healer. Often people can't see an energy blockage or they're looking for an obvious in-your-face solution. **Often a shift in perception brings in helpful information for awareness and forward movement.**

4. Be Vulnerable

There's a lot of conversations about the benefits of being vulnerable, thanks to Brené Brown and other self-help experts. Vulnerability is a harder muscle to strengthen because It's easier to understand intellectually, rather than emotionally. The visual of Louie being vulnerable is etched in my mind and heart and helps me form deeper connections by being vulnerable with family and friends. It's hard to "do" vulnerability. When Louie feels joy holding a bully stick with his paws and lays on his back smiling, he affirms that vulnerability involves BEing exposed and receptive. When Louie rolls on his back to offer his belly for me to pet him or while he's playing with a toy, he's able to fully feel his bliss. If he needs help removing something from his paw, like a prickly twig, he rolls over or lifts his leg to receive help. He doesn't resist. **Vulnerability allows enough of the defense systems we've built to soften, so we can feel safe enough to receive guidance or inspiration.**

5. Catch is Always a New Game

Louie and I play catch a few times a day. Every day, my best friend plays the game as though it's the first time he's ever played it. I can sense he feels a fresh, new sense of wonder each time we toss around his treat or stuffed animal. He hops and gallops with breaths of pure excitement. The daily minutia of life can take the fun out of many blessings we're presented with each day. I often felt that I was caught in a daily grind working in corporate America, or even in my dating life. **Louie reminds me that each day is a brand-new day. He's pointed out that whatever energy we engage with each day is unique and presents a new opportunity for adventure, interaction, and fun.**

6. Unconditional Love Exists

Of course, my family and close friends deeply love me and support me. Louie's love is special to me because **Louie's love for me has no conditions. It's a powerful deep feeling and bond.** I have yet to meet someone who looks at me with such love as my little Louie, and that's helped to root me at my core. It's not really about what I do, it's about me just being me. Although, he loves me that much more when I give him his favorite treat.

Is having a dog a lot of work and can it be costly at times? Yes. Take a breath. What is the cost of not listening to your heart? Hurricane Sandy—a natural disaster—shook me up enough to realize what I was withholding in my life. My prayer was answered with the help of all the amazing gifts my Louie has shared with me. Those treats and love cannot be measured or quantified. I'm filled with gratitude for his nine pounds of friendship and love.

If you ever felt called to get a dog and talked yourself out of it, consider that it might open you to deeper ground in inviting more into your life—especially play, being vulnerable, speaking your truth, sensing what's around you differently and feeling unconditional love. There's no time like the present.

Lorraine Giordano

Lorraine Giordano is an intuitive energy healer shifting the way women connect to down there. Lorraine is passionate about sharing ways for women to connect to their own healing and creative energy, and highlighting opportunities to bridge the gap from disease to finding their personal healthy way in their daily life. She previously worked in the financial industry developing financial software products and experienced many health challenges over two decades.

Due to the threat of losing her uterus in 2008, she realized how much she did not know about her body, especially her female reproductive organs. Not willing to give up her uterus, she put Operation Save Uterus into action and learned how to reclaim her health. As a holistic energy healer, with her uterus intact, she now helps women connect to their own healing ability and understand the importance and power of down there.

Lorraine is an Usui Reiki Master and certified in Quantum Energy Transformation, Quantum Touch, and Integrated Energy Therapy. Lorraine won the Best of Award 2015 by Thumbtack for Reiki Masters in NYC and in 2013 and 2016 she won a bronze Stevie Award for Women Helping Women. Her newsletter has won the Constant Contact All-Star Award the past three years. She contributed to the Huffington Post and she is also a co-author of the international bestseller, *The Grandmother Legacies*. She is the host on *The Womb Happy Hour* radio show on VoiceAmerica Health & Wellness. In 2018, she expanded her healing practice, Sage of Clear Spaces, to help clear the energy of people's homes and offices in person and remotely.

Social Media:
Facebook: **https://facebook.com/inspiredtohealth**
Twitter: https://twitter.com/inspire2health
Instagram: https://instagram.com/sageofclearspaces

EASTER'S STORY
BY AERIOL ASCHER

More than any other situation or any other thing in my life, the relationships I have with my dogs have been the most reliable, the most comforting, and the most unconditional source of love I have had. They manage to anchor themselves deeply into our hearts and our lives, and they shape our lives and family structures. These relationships with my pets have taught me more about behavior and given me more insights about personality than all my studies of metaphysical healing, philosophy, art, and science.

The best way to describe it is that the animals represent my connection to the magic of nature. They offer unconditional love and acceptance in a way that I have never been able to recreate in my "human" world. Each of my dogs has taught volumes of life lessons through our experiences together.

When she was alive, my grandmother had urged me to tell Easter's magical story. After all these years I finally sat down to write the story of how Easter got his name. I hope that it will help me not only to heal my grief of his loss, but also to make my grandmother, who wrote children stories, proud of me. I also hope that those reading it will be inspired to write their stories and heal their hearts.

Here is the story of how Easter chose me:

It was about four in the morning on Easter of 2004 when I felt someone licking my ear. "Stop it, Ruby! Go back to bed... I'm tired." I mumbled half asleep and I lazily turned to see that it was not in fact Ruby, and it was not even Maxx, who was known for this sort of thing. It was a little white dog with sparkly black eyes, cockeyed ears, and a smiling heart that oozed pure joy.

Now mind you, Easter weighed about seven pounds and was not only just in my house... but in my bed! That is right–he made his way into my backyard, up the back steps, through the dog door, through the house, into my bedroom and somehow shimmied all the way up into the bed!

Easter seemed like the perfect addition to my family pack at "Doggtoppia" which is the pet name I gave my home. At this time in my life I was doing a lot of dog sitting, plus I had my own fur babies Maxx and Ruby who were four years old. Honestly, my backyard probably smelled like the doggie Underground Railroad, and he just fit right in.

I had Easter for almost a week when I overheard a man talking at a shop near my house about how his teenage stepdaughter who was acting out admitted that she took a dog she had found in Fresno and smuggled him to her mother's house in her duffle bag on the Greyhound bus. She had been hiding the dog under her bed for days, but there was a toddler in their house who kept messing with the little stow away, freaking him out. Apparently, our little man had one too many terrifying run ins with the toddler and made a break for it!

It seemed that my surprise magical love affair had ended. Reluctantly, I gave up the dog to the man to bring home to his rebellious stepdaughter. By this time I had already grown quite attached, so this was not an easy decision to make, but I wanted to do the right thing. Easter blended in so well with Maxx and Ruby that it was hard to let go. Life finally felt so complete in our happy Doggtopia bubble! But if the tables were turned, I would have wanted him back too.

Not to worry, however–later that evening while sitting on the couch watching TV with Maxx, Ruby, and the cat, Aengus, we heard a pop through the dog door and Easter came trotting in. Just like that, he came in, plopped down, and made himself right at home.

The next day I walked down the street to the neighbor's house with Easter under my arm and handed him over once again.

But wouldn't you know it, later that night here he came popping through though the doggie door. This went on for five or six times. I would march down the street and hand him over and several hours later he would burrow through what must have been a one-way hole in the fence and back through the dog door once again!

On what must have been the seventh time, I marched down to the neighbor's house and this time was greeted by the mother.

"I'm keeping my dog" I blurted out with the certainty of a mama bear. The woman sighed and spoke so sweetly to me. She explained the daughter brought the dog without their knowing and we agreed that the daughter could keep the dog for one more night in order to say good-bye and that she would march down to my house with him the next morning and he would then stay with me. I left him with the mother around four in the afternoon.

What do you think happened next? That's right; just after dark as I was washing the dinner dishes, I hear the pop of the dog door and our little lover-man came prancing in. That time he was home for good.

I have never in my life come across such a loving, adaptable, and joyful creature. He had all his teeth removed because there was decay from before he found me. I remember thinking he would not be able to survive it! But I have to say, it did not even slow him down at dinnertime! His tongue poked out the side of his mouth giving him a delightfully deranged and utterly gleeful expression.

Easter never minded being the middle man between Ruby and Maxx. He was comfortable being a protector if Maxx was ever napping, and he was also quit patient when Miss Ruby would get snippy in her neurotic sort of Miss Ruby way. My beautiful little family stuck together like glue.

Easter was so strong after Maxx died in May 2016. He made sure that everyone got cuddles to heal their grieving hearts. When Easter's groomer brought over the last of a litter her dog had shortly after Maxx passed, it seemed a natural fit to bring Ziggy into our fold. Easter rose to the occasion and was a delightful big brother and showed Ziggy the ins and outs of dealing with Ruby in no time.

It seemed our blissful little family moved on, but just a year after losing Maxx, Miss Ruby left us. Easter and his blessed heart was a pillar of strength once again and was there for Ziggy. He helped him adjust to changes after we adopted an older rescue dog named Dali.

The day I lost Easter (Sept 2, 2018) was perhaps one of the most traumatic events in my life since the day my grandmother passed in July 2007. Yes, the passing of Maxx and Ruby was hard, but this was almost devastating. He had stopped eating the day before and I knew something was wrong with him. He kept coming to me that morning and trying to get my attention, looking longingly into my eyes. I picked him up and just sat and rocked him slowly how he liked to be cradled. Unexpectedly and without struggle he gasped and he passed gently in my arms. I was beside myself.

It is hard to believe he is gone. He was just yapping in his raspy little bark to have me rush to the bedroom and help him down the doggie stairs we put up to help him get into our bed, which was always way too high for him to jump into. Once a friend heard him do that and she asked if we had a bird. I asked her to wait for a moment and I ran to the back of the house and set our little man on the ground and he went tearing down the hallway to greet her. I heard gales of laughter as she witnessed him leaping and bounding towards her. I love that little clown. I used to call him our court jester. Maxx was the King, and of course her highness Princess Ruby-doo.

Time moves on and I noticed how the dog politics changed. Ziggy sweetly and steadfastly took over the role of protector, and wore the crown handed down from my precious Easter after the changing of the guards. Never to fear, Ziggy and Dali would have plenty of adventures and dynamics to navigate, since just a short three months after the passing of my beloved Easter I was prompted by my guides to visit the local animal shelter.

Twinkie entered our life like a force of nature, and believe it or not my **connection to Easter and the love he taught me has never been stronger!**

The connection I feel with these creatures is incredible, and their impact upon my life is profound. They teach me everything I need to know about unconditional love, loyalty, and service. Their devotion gives me purpose and meaning at times when my own confidence wears thin, and their emotional support in both good times and bad make this chaotic world make sense, even if just for a moment.

As I fumble for the words to tell Easter's legacy story, I cannot express how huge the heart was in that tiny little creature! Rest in Peace my little one. I love you so much. You brought me so much joy. Please tell Maxx and Miss Ruby I love them. Say hello to Grandma and Grandpa for me. Please know that I would not trade these eighteen years with you for anything in the world. I feel so very lucky that you chose me. I will meet you all on the other side of the rainbow bridge on that day, some years from now, when I too shall return home, my beloved. I will be greeted on the other side of the rainbow bridge by a couch full of glorious lap dogs, and I will feel nothing but unconditional love.

The legacy of love I want to share with you, dear reader, is that each of us can share love and lead with love. Part of the reason Easter had such an impact on all that he met was his bright, joyful, and determined love. Be willing to share your bright, joyful, and determined love with those around you. Be willing to carry that legacy forward.

Aeriol Ascher

Aeriol Ascher is an Author, Speaker, Teacher, Holistic Healing Master, Intuitive Guide, and Voice & Presence Coach. She has been in the field of self-care and personal development for 25+ years. Before closing the doors in 2017, her Holistic Healing Practice: Reiki Angel Intuitive Arts was voted Best Day Spa in Silicon Valley by the San Jose Mercury News, and her signature Reiki Angel Massage was voted best massage four times.

Aeriol empowers her clients with tools to increase body awareness, hone intuition, and connect to their highest self so they can confidently show up, speak up, and stand out in their personal and professional lives. She has a passion for facilitating group healing experiences that awaken self-awareness, inspire growth, and create a safe and sacred learning environment for spiritual awakening, personal empowerment, and fun.

An advocate for self-expression and women in leadership, Aeriol loves to assist her clients to align with their most authentic selves so they can embody their most powerful presence and let their souls shine. Aeriol is available for speaking engagements, group and individual training, coaching, and private healing sessions both live or via video conferencing technology.

Aeriol lives in San Jose, CA with her fur family, consisting her dogs Ziggy, Twinkie, Dali and their 15-year-old cat Aengus. (photo with rescue dog Dali)

More about Aeriol: **www.AeriolAscher.com**
Healing Practice: **www.SomaSoundTherapy.com**
Podcast: **www.HealingBodyMindandSoul.com**

Social Links:
www.facebook.com/askaeriol
www.facebook.com/somasoundtherapy
www.instagram.com/askaeriol/
www.twitter.com/askaeriol
www.youtube.com/user/ReikiAngelMassage
www.linkedin.com/in/aeriolascher/

NEIGHBORHOOD LESSONS:
GERALYN AND CHANCE
BY LORRAINE GIORDANO

The last time I saw Geralyn was at the end of August 2016. I took Louie, my Maltipoo—part Maltese, part Poodle—out for his afternoon walk. Three houses down, Geralyn was sitting outside on her porch, wearing a patterned dress, enjoying the beautiful, sunny day. Louie and I walked up the stairs to her porch, where she sat on her plastic white outdoor chair, eating fried chicken wings from a white Styrofoam container. She loved Louie and he was quite fond of her. She offered him some chicken and he gladly grabbed it from her greasy fingers, then trotted to her front door, where he sniffed and whined, eager to go inside to say hello and hang out with her dog, Handsome. During this visit, Handsome would stay inside on the second floor and miss the porch gathering.

Geralyn didn't have children and was never married. We both shared a love for dogs. In the eighteen months since I'd been her neighbor, she told me about the different dogs she had and how much they meant to her. Geralyn was so fond of Louie that she ended up getting a Maltipoo from the same breeder in Newark, New Jersey, where I got Louie. Geralyn named Louie's bigger and fatter brother, Handsome. These furry relatives looked more like cousins than brothers. At the time Geralyn got Handsome, she was having a difficult time walking due to severe pain in her knees. She fell a few times and her extra weight prevented her from moving around easily. Geralyn and Handsome didn't go for walks outside, although they spent a lot of time inside together playing and loving each other with hugs and kisses. Handsome did all his business on wee-wee pads. As they spent most of their time together, they shared a deep love for each other.

Like other neighbors on the block, from time to time I helped Geralyn carry groceries inside, picked up frozen dinners and eggs at the store, and carried Handsome downstairs from her house to the car for vet or the groomer visits. Geralyn enjoyed chatting about the changes on the block during the six decades living in the same house she grew up in. She also liked talking about what is was like being a teacher's aide. Of course, we talked a lot about our dogs and other characters in the neighborhood. She seemed to know every dog's story, even if they lived blocks away. Her eyes lit up sharing about Handsome and other dogs she had or had a soft spot for.

The last time I heard Geralyn's voice–a couple of weeks after we visited on her porch–she left me a voicemail to let me know she was feeling better after having a terrible stomach virus for a few days. I got caught up with Labor Day weekend activities and didn't call her back. I wish I had. I'm not sure if it would have changed anything. I'll always wonder.

Geralyn passed away in her apartment on Labor Day weekend of 2016. She was sixty-seven years old. She is survived by her father, who is in his nineties, and her stepsister. Although her life wasn't acknowledged in an obituary, she left a legacy of love and opened the chance for unique connections.

Seasons have come and gone. I still think of my friend Geralyn, walking with Louie past her beautifully renovated house that's now occupied with a young family. **My neighbor left an imprint on my heart and mind. Geralyn's house stands as a reminder to me of kindness, love, and the gift of life each day.**

As sad as her passing was, there are many miracles worth mentioning in her honor.

The Police Officer

The police officer who told me about her passing that Tuesday evening in September asked me four separate times if I would take in Handsome. Each time I said no, feeling sick to my stomach. A couple of months before Geralyn passed she had knee surgery and asked me if I would take in Handsome if anything happened to her. At the time I thought it was a strange question to ask because she was just having knee surgery. I told her I wouldn't be able to afford another dog because of how much I travelled. The officer seemed especially concerned for Handsome and went out of his way to keep bringing up the opportunity to give Handsome to me. The last time Officer Jake asked me that evening, after most of the neighbors had gone inside and the ambulance and most of the police cars drove away, he made a point of bringing Handsome over to me. My neighbor, Jada, sat with me on the stoop outside as we tried to come up with possible solutions to save Handsome.

Louie's Dog Walker/Aunt

Feeling terrible, depressed, and haunted by the look in the eyes of the police officer and feeling like I could hear Geralyn silently scream, *Take the dog, Lorraine, save Handsome Lorraine*, I called my friend Ro, the dog whisperer of Weehawken, New Jersey, and Louie's dog walker and aunt. When I go away, Ro's place is Louie's home away from home. I asked Ro if she knew anyone who would want a dog and shared that the police officer said Handsome would wind up in the pound in Newark. Ro said that was a kill shelter. I happened to mention the police officer's name, Jake, and she said she knew Jake very well. She told me to call the station and tell Jack that she and I would pick up Handsome in the morning and to not bring Handsome to Newark.

My Cousin in Texas

That night, in a moment of clarity, I remembered my cousin Linna, who lives in Frisco, Texas, was interested in getting a dog like Louie. Worried about Handsome's fate, I called Linna right away. She said she was going to be in New York City later that week with her two daughters and husband to visit her father-in-law who was undergoing major surgery. After I sent a couple of pictures of Handsome, she said she would figure out how to fly him home with her. With a new possible home for Handsome, after another phone call to Ro, I called the police station again and asked Officer Jake to bring Handsome to my house. Within the hour, Handsome was with Louie and me.

Judy the Neighbor

Handsome and I slept for ten minutes that night. Louie wasn't pleased that his brother was crashing at our place. The following morning, as my roommate spotted Handsome on her way out the door to work, she shot me the look of horror. As a result, I had to find a place for Handsome for the next few days. Ro couldn't board Handsome because he wasn't neutered, and it would cause problems with her dog and the other dogs she took care of. Desperate, and in a frazzled state, I asked my neighbor Judy, an older single woman with a love of playing the piano, if she would take in Handsome for the week until I could bring him over to my cousin. Thankfully she agreed, and they became fast friends! Judy and I both enjoyed giggling while watching Handsome and Louie running around together in my backyard.

Jada the Neighbor

My other neighbor, Jada, is a talented artist, mom, and big lover of dogs, cats, and all animals. As a pet foster care provider, she has gone way beyond the call of duty to help find animals loving homes. She wanted to take Handsome in, but it was too complicated with her cats. To get Handsome on the plane, he needed a checkup and a note from the vet. Frequently offering to help with texts and calls, Jada gave me a ride to the vet to handle all the paperwork for Handsome to fly the friendly skies. Fortunately, Handsome made it safely to Texas with his new family.

A New Life in Frisco, Texas

My cousin's family decided to change Handsome's name to Chance. It was truly by chance that they added a new member to their family.

Although I'll always think of him as Handsome, they gave him a beautiful new chance at life. **Geralyn's wish for her dog to be taken care of came true! Chance lives a well-loved, fun, and glamourous life in Frisco, Texas.** One of the best gifts of Chance's new family was his friendship with Benji, my cousin's dog of many moons. It took Benji a little while to warm up to Chance, but the old timer ultimately gave the newbie a chance. They had fun running around and playing with my cousin's daughters for a year and a half before Benji sadly passed away due to kidney issues in the winter of 2018. From what I hear, Chance misses his best friend. Even though Chance is deeply loved and well-cared for, I wondered if losing his friend stirred up hard memories of losing his mom, Geralyn.

At a time when there is such divisiveness, polarity of judgements, and opinions on so many different topics across the country, the story of Geralyn's wish and the miracle of Handsome finding a new home gives me hope in the goodness of people from different walks of life, with different experiences and opinions. It affirms for me the power of neighbors coming together with kindness in their hearts to help someone in the community.

Although Geralyn is gone, she is not forgotten. She made a difference.

May Geralyn and Chance's story of love and friendship serve as a reminder that:

1) The love of animals and love shared between owner and animal can help bridge perceived differences between people and animals.
2) Whether you have a dog or not, if a problem seems too challenging or overwhelming – ask for help. Extra hands, minds, and hearts are available to assist and can create miraculous solutions.
3) Tomorrow is not promised–share your appreciation and love with your family, friends, and animals each day!

Chance (Handsome)   Louise

Lorraine Giordano

Lorraine Giordano is an intuitive energy healer shifting the way women connect to down there. Lorraine is passionate about sharing ways for women to connect to their own healing and creative energy, and highlighting opportunities to bridge the gap from disease to finding their personal healthy way in their daily life. She previously worked in the financial industry developing financial software products and experienced many health challenges over two decades.

Due to the threat of losing her uterus in 2008, she realized how much she didn't know about her body, especially her female reproductive organs. Not willing to give up her uterus, she put Operation Save Uterus into action and learned how to reclaim her health. As a holistic energy healer, with her uterus intact, she now helps women connect to their own healing ability and understand the importance and power of down there.

Lorraine is an Usui Reiki Master and certified in Quantum Energy Transformation, Quantum Touch and Integrated Energy Therapy. Lorraine won the Best of Award 2015 by Thumbtack for Reiki Masters in NYC and in 2013 and 2016 she won a bronze Stevie Award for Women Helping Women. Her newsletter has won the Constant Contact All-Star Award the past three years. She contributed to the Huffington Post and she is also a co-author of the international bestseller, The Grandmother Legacies. She is the host on The Womb Happy Hour radio show on VoiceAmerica Health & Wellness. In 2018, she expanded her healing practice, Sage of Clear Spaces, to help clear the energy of people's homes and offices in person and remotely.

Social Media:
Facebook: **https://facebook.com/inspiredtohealth**
Twitter: https://twitter.com/inspire2health
Instagram: https://instagram.com/sageofclearspaces

SECTION 2:

Feline Forever Friends

PATCHES THE CHRISTMAS CAT
BY REBECCA HALL GRUYTER

Is it possible for a little creature who sleeps a lot and does not speak to be an incredible being who has an impact on every life he touches?

Yes! That was my Patches...here is his story.

I had my heart set on I getting a cat...someday, someday, someday. My coworkers knew this, and they heard all my reasons why I never felt quite ready.

One December, our leadership team went on a business trip and took a limo to Union Square in San Francisco, living it up with mimosas, brunch, and holiday shopping.

As we passed Neiman Marcus, we saw these kittens playing in the windowsill. I found myself staring at one of them, with black and white spots like a cow's hide. He was just so playful that I kind of fell in love with him. My coworker was eyeing me, and said, "Rebecca, now is your moment."

To set the stage...did I mention we'd had mimosas? And, being in the spirit of the season, I was wearing a bright red Christmas sweater with a zillion tiny chimes on it, I had a bell around my neck as a necklace, and I wore a Christmas hat and big, old Christmas earrings.

My coworker nudged me and said, "You need this cat. We're gonna make this happen." I had reservations.

"This is a business trip, I can't...it's not the right time..."

"Oooh, no," she said, and this apparently became her mission. So, I did finally go inside and talk with them about wanting to adopt this cat. They stared at me and my chimes, and undoubtedly smelled alcohol on me. They were clearly stalling. I began to feel uncertain and realized that I really wanted this little guy. Before I knew it, my coworker came to the rescue, and as far as I could tell just bullied them into it. We walked out with this little kitten in a box. There are company photos still around where you will see us and the cat carrying case standing outside the limo at Union Square.

Then it dawned on us that the limo driver was not going to let the cat into his car. We all ganged up on him, and bribed him by offering to let him name the cat. He finally relented, and named him Boots (we later decided on Patches, which we liked better—the limo driver would never know). In the limo, as we were laughing, having a good time, and talking about our adventures of the day, I took Patches out of his case and sat him on my lap. He curled right up and promptly fell asleep as comfortable as can be, never afraid. All of us fell in love with him.

And so, Patches came home.

Another thing I had not thought of was my landlady, who was against cats. But Patches even charmed her! She would pick him up and place him in the window to watch the passersby. The neighbors began to get to know him, too, and they would come up to the windowsill to pet and play with him. The neighborhood kids loved him, and he was so friendly with every one of them. He loved life, loved people, and loved children. They called him the Cow Cat and I was the Cat Lady.

I called him my Christmas Cat. He loved Christmas—really, he did! He loved Christmas music, and whenever I would wear that sweater with the chimes he would get excited. Ir felt as though that was a really special moment for him, like it was for me.

There was something so special about Patches. I believe he could read people well, because even those who were not "cat people" always felt safe with him. A friend would be upset and come over to visit me, and Patches would come along to curl up next to them or on their lap. Actually, I'm sure he thought they were visiting him! It was as if he understood that they needed some extra love in those moments. He seemed to know whenever I was upset, and would hop up and sit beside me to comfort me.

Patches had this little squished-up nose that he had some sinus problems as well as other health issues at a young age. So, we were in and out of the vet's office quite often trying to resolve these. The vet and all the technicians just loved him; everybody seemed to be touched by him on a deep level. He mattered to them.

With so many health challenges, there were many times when I was prepared to be told that Patches would not make it. But, he was such a fighter, and he would always pull through against the odds, over and over again. It was truly a remarkable thing about him that has had a deep impact on me; he loved life so much, and he lived well beyond any life expectancy he had ever been given.

Mr. Patch also had quite his own personality. For example, he was very good at getting attention. If he felt like he was being neglected, he would make it a point to pass by me, limping as if he'd injured one of his front paws! I'd hop up and go to him (the first few times in a little bit of a panic because he had so many health issues).

"Oh, my goodness, are you okay?" Once he got his hug and love and attention, he'd go back to walking normally.

Patches also seemed to believe he was a dog. During this time I got married, so my new husband, Andrew, Patches, and I became a family. Andrew had not quite believed me when I told him that this cat would play tug-of-war with me, fetch toys that were tossed to him, and come when I called him, until he experienced Patches himself. He would even greet us at the door when we came home with great joy.

Andrew also was skeptical of the "limping tactic," until one day he saw Patches walk through the room forlornly and dramatically limping, favoring his front right leg. Andrew ignored him, but as Patches left the room he looked around the corner to see that the little furry imp was perfectly all right. Andrew resumed his seat in the chair and, sure enough, Patches limped by again, on the right leg this time!

"It's like he forgot which foot he was limping on," Andrew told me later. "And then he chose the wrong one and came limping back, and I knew I was on to him!"

Over the years Patches' vet would talk to us about him and his impact on others. When it became, as it sadly does with our precious animals, toward the end of Patches' time, he was struggling and not smelling his best. So, we played Christmas music and spent a lot of time with him. People actually came to visit him and comfort him, and if he was not in the room you could be sure that he would slowly and painfully come down the stairs to them, like it was his job to lift THEIR spirits. I was so touched and moved by those who made a special trip to come and hold Patches, pet him, be with him, and thank him. He had a huge impact on many people.

There was no question that Patches was a therapy cat.Every friend, family member, neighbor, caregiver and cat sitter who crossed his path would share that being with him uplifted their spirits, calmed them, and had them feeling loved. People would call me after a time with Patches and let me know what he had done or how he had just understood them when they were having a really bad day.

It's no surprise that the Christmas Cat left a lasting legacy to me, Andrew, and all of the people whose lives were touched by this little being.

Just thinking about how Patches brought out the playful and impulsive part of me from that first moment I saw him in front of Neiman Marcus helps me remember to lighten up when things seem serious or overwhelming, or I want to say "no" instead of "yes." I had the privilege of experiencing what unconditional love looks like, and how sometimes we don't even need words to let someone know we are by their side comforting them with our presence, assurance, care, and understanding. I believe I might have learned that drawing attention to ourselves is not always such a bad thing.

I hope this Christmas brings you a special gift that uplifts your heart and spirit...that brings out your lighter and joy-filled spirit. I hope it reminds you to love life and know that you too have a powerful impact on all that cross your path.

Rebecca Hall Gruyter

Rebecca Hall Gruyter is a Global Influencer, #1 International Best-Selling Author, and Compiler, Publisher, Radio Show Host (reaching over 1 million listeners on 7 networks), and an Empowerment Leader that wants to help you reach more people. She has built multiple platforms to help experts reach more people. These platforms include: Radio, TV, books, magazines, the Speaker Talent Search, and Live Events, creating a powerful promotional reach of over 10 million!

Rebecca is the CEO of RHG Media Productions (which includes the RHG TV Network with over 30 weekly programs and Publishing Arm—that has helped 200+ authors become best sellers!) She is the owner of Your Purpose Driven Practice and the creator of the Speaker Talent Search.

Rebecca has personally contributed to 20+ published books, multiple magazines, and has been quoted in Major Media: The Huffington Post, ABC, CBS, NBC, Fox, and Thrive Global. She now helps experts get quoted in major media too.

Today, she wants to share with you: How you too, can be seen, be heard and SHINE!

www.YourPurposeDrivenPractice.com
www.RHGTVNetwork.com
www.SpeakerTalentSearch.com
Rebecca@YourPurposeDrivenPractice.com

Social Media:
www.EmpoweringWomenTransformingLives (radio show)

Facebook:
www.facebook.com/rhallgruyter
www.facebook.com/pages/Rebecca-Hall-Gruyter/442052769207010
LinkedIn: **www.linkedin.com/pub/rebecca-hall-gruyter/9/266/280**
Twitter: **www.twitter.com/Rebeccahgruyter**
Instagram: RHGTVNetwork

CONFESSIONS OF A CRAZY CAT LADY
BY TRACY DIETLEIN

Once upon a time, in a land not so far away, there lived a forty-something princess, (*that would be me*), who was single, (GASP!), childless, (GASP!), and still searching for her happily ever after.

Now, unlike your typical fairy tale princess, I suck at housework, my singing voice is atrocious, my mother is alive and well, and the only beasts in my life are my two freakishly large cat-princes, Buster and Rocky. And quite frankly, they can't sing either.

At this point in my life, I find myself stuck in a category that is much too often overlooked. I somehow (*theoretically*) missed the cutoff date for marriage, children, and any other dream I may have once wished upon a star. Prince Charming seems more interested in a younger model, and rather than going to extremes to vie for his attention, this damsel in distress would much rather curl up on the couch with a family-size bag of *Lay's* potato chips and watch multiple episodes of *Dateline*.

And I am usually not alone in this scenario. I am often accompanied by not one, but two—yes you read that correctly—two cats, who are *way* more interested in the potato chips than who murdered the woman at the lake.

I find pets to be an important part of people's lives. Let's face it; we live in a world where it is socially acceptable for a dog to be your best friend and a cat to be your closest confidant.

HOWEVER, if you are a single woman, over the age of forty with one or, *god forbid*, multiple cats...you are automatically deemed crazy. Case in point:

- A woman in her twenties or thirties with one or more cats = **Socially Acceptable**.
- A woman of any age with a spouse and/or children with one or more cats = **Socially Acceptable**.
- A woman in a committed relationship with one or more cats = **Moderately Acceptable**.
- A single woman in her forties who lives alone with one or more cats = **Crazy Cat Lady**.

This is so not fair! Why are we labeled as *Crazy Cat Ladies* simply for being of a certain age and single? And why does this only seem to pertain to women? Think about it, you never hear of any *Crazy Cat Men*. In fact, a single man over forty with a cat is viewed as adorable and desired. A single woman over forty with a cat...she's just plain sad, with a *hint* of pathetic.

I have lived alone for over twenty years now, and I cannot imagine not having a cat in my life...or two.

When I first moved out on my own, it was lonely, and I was only able to see our family cat on weekends when I had visitation rights from my parents; it was like I was on parole and only allowed supervised visits! Therefore, although I was afraid of the responsibility, I decided to get a cat of my own.

That was when Bill came into my life. The sweetest, most loving cat in the world.

Bill was three years old when I met him. He was a delightful orange tabby who had been rescued from an abusive household. He had major dental issues from trying to chew his way through a barbed wire fence to escape his former circumstances. I remember seeing him at the pet store and immediately fell in love with him, then and there. There was just something about this cat. He had such a horrible upbringing, yet he appeared to be so full of love and hope.

Despite our instant attraction, I did not adopt him. I was fearful of all his health issues and the added responsibility, so I left the store empty handed, and heavy-hearted.

I went back to see him the next week, but to my dismay, he was gone. However, when I mentioned Bill's name to the adoption representative, she lit up like a Christmas tree, and a few days later, to my surprise, she showed up at my door with the cat in tow.

And that is when I rescued Bill.

And in return, Bill rescued me.

And we lived happily for the next ten years. He was a wonderful cat— so loving and affectionate. He stole my heart and introduced me to an unconditional love I did not know was possible. Throughout the rest of my twenties and into my thirties, Bill remained the one constant male in my life, and even though I was often confronted with the *"why aren't you married"* and *"what's wrong with you"* interrogation sequence from others, having that cat in my life gave me a sense of serenity and security, in spite of my perceived shortcomings.

He was all I needed.

And then, just like that, he was taken away from me. Our time was cut short and my heart was broken into a million pieces, as he succumbed to an unexpected illness and passed away quite suddenly. I was absolutely devastated. I could not imagine my life without Bill. Where else was I going to find that kind of love and devotion, that kind of tender companionship? He was so special to me, and even though he is in cat heaven now, he still owns all those pieces of my heart that broke the day I had no choice but to put him down.

After Bill died, everyone tried to convince me to get another cat, which I could not even fathom. I was never going to find a cat as amazing as Bill. Yet, after some time, I have to admit, my house felt very empty, and I was overcome with loneliness.

My friend Erin convinced me to go to a pet store with her to "look" at some rescue kittens that were found along the side of a freeway. I told her I was not going to adopt, but agreed to go along for the ride.

I think we all know where this is going, because...

The rest is history, as that was the day I rescued my two big-boned princes.

And they rescued me right back.

After viewing the assortment of overly cute kittens at the pet store, I set my sights on one cat in particular named Digit. He was called this because he had six claws on every paw. He was like a Clydesdale in the form of a cat! I immediately fell in love with Digit, and began the adoption process. Nearing completion, the adoption representative said that since I am single and work so much, it might be a good idea to consider getting Digit a buddy. I scoffed at the idea. After all, at the time, I was a woman in my mid-thirties–I could not have multiple cats. What would people think? *The horror! The horror!*

But...

There was another cat in the bunch that was tugging at my heart strings–it was Digit's brother, Rocky. Still hesitant, I was about to leave with just the one cat. However, when I was told the second cat would be half off, I ended up leaving the store with *two* cats! What can I say, I can't resist a good deal!

And so, a new love story began.

After bringing both kittens home, I was a nervous wreck. What was I going to do with *two* cats? And again, what would people think? Single woman outnumbered by cats? This is the stuff Greek tragedies are made of!

I renamed Digit "Buster", as my beloved San Francisco Giants had just won the *World Series*, so to celebrate, Buster's namesake became that of future Hall of Famer, Buster Posey. I was going to rename Rocky after one of the Giants as well...but, he just looked like a Rocky. And luckily, our relationship through the years has been anything but.

As my two precious kittens grew into two, jumbo-sized cats, my love for them expanded as well. These two cats make me crazy, and yet, they make me laugh and smile all at the same time. And sure, they take the occasional dump on my carpet, throw up on my bed, (while I'm in it), use my $800 couch as the world's largest scratching post, (along with the rest of my living room furniture), and sleep on my spleen, bladder and throat, respectively, every night, (that's over 50 pounds of love, by the way), I adore them more than words can say. I just do not care anymore what people think. They make me happy, and that is all that matters.

And truly, that is all that should matter.

And so, I have come to embrace my *Crazy Cat Lady* status, and in fact, I wear the title proudly, like a badge of honor. It should not matter what my gender, age or marital status is. I have two companions that are there when I wake up in the morning and are there to greet me at the door when I come home from work at night. They give me a purpose beyond myself, and keep me going when the world sometimes becomes a very dark place.

They truly did rescue me from a life of loneliness.

And when people say to me, usually in some derogatory manner, *"at least you have your cats"*, I keep my head held high and say, "Yes I do!"

I AM A CRAZY CAT LADY – **HEAR ME MEOW!**

And she lived and loved unconditionally ever after.

Tracy Dietlein

Tracy Dietlein is the Senior Marketing Manager of a premier shopping center in Walnut Creek, California. Although Tracy has always had big dreams of becoming a full-time writer, she has spent the last twenty years at the mall dealing with numerous cranky shoppers, has seen Santa naked one too many times, has yelled at the Easter Bunny for smoking on set, and was once viciously attacked by an unruly mob at a community parade while dressed as Nutmeg the Squirrel, the mall's short-lived mascot.

Despite her questionable years in public service, Tracy is a very creative person who specializes in strategic planning, while maintaining a sense of control and a sense of humor.

Well...at least a sense of humor.

Tracy is a self-proclaimed *Crazy Cat Lady*, as her roommates include two jumbo-sized lions named Buster and Rocky, and she pretends to be an "age appropriate" princess on the side, sharing her stories of love, survival, and humiliation in her personal blog, *Forty Tales*.

www.FortyTales.com
www.facebook.com/40Tales
www.instagram.com/40tales
www.pinterest.com/40tales

LESSONS FROM THE "TA-DA" CAT AND MOCHA BEAN
BY REBECCA HALL GRUYTER

There is a real power in being willing to receive whatever may come along with playfulness and humbleness. Life is much more fun when we meet it with celebration, and even choose to SHINE!

There are going to be those moments in your life when you will be surprised, challenged, or pushed a little outside of your comfort zone—even feel a bit embarrassed. We have all been there. What do you do, for example, when you attend an event and someone comes up to take your picture or asks for a selfie? In those moments, we can have a tendency to do the "duck away" to move out of the way of that person or scramble to get out of sight.

"No, I don't want a picture! My hair's a mess; I don't look good today! No, I don't want to speak up or be interviewed! What if I make a mistake? I don't know what to say!"

These may be what we say or the things that are running through our minds in a loop. Ducking away from being seen and heard holds us back from bringing forth what is ours to share with the world.

Do you know what I have learned? They are going to take your picture anyway–and post it! I also know that the "duck away" pictures will NEVER look good. We end up with weird expressions or hands waving around awkwardly to cover our face, or our eyes are half-shut.

It's better to plan to respond to those kinds of situations on purpose, with purpose, and to take center stage and have fun. Smile, lean in, and receive. Your picture will be so much better, because your energy is raised and you are open and willing to SHINE.

Just throw up your hands and say, "TA-DA!"

Nina the TA-DA Cat

What do I mean by "TA-DA?"

Well, I learned this from my cat: sweet, little Nina. She was a beautiful tortoiseshell, her soft fur speckled with flecks of orange, black, and white. Nina was demure and very timid. She didn't even meow or yowl–she chirped!

She was afraid of other people, even my friends or family who were with us often; she would shrink away, or she would walk into the room and stay perfectly still for a really long time. She would just freeze up, as if she thought if she was still then no one would see her. It was as though she was saying, "I'm invisible. Nothing to see here." When I would go to pick her up, she would go completely limp like a ragdoll in my arms, still believing she was being invisible.

This is why it was so surprising, and memorable, when Nina would come into the room with just my husband and I. She did not just come in; she would make an entrance! She would strut in, tail high, majestically as only cats can do, right into the middle of the room. Then she would stop, sit tall, and look regally around the room and at us. If she were a human, she would be raising her arms high in the air with a sassy stance, announcing: "Ta Da! I'm here!" It made us laugh every time. After a few moments, if she did not feel she was getting our attention, she would chirp (remember, not meow) until we acknowledged her. Once we did, she would just get up and go on with her cat business.

Now, *that* is the way to be seen, heard, and SHINE!

Nina is no longer with us, but she remains in my heart as the "TA-DA Cat". She taught me a powerful lesson, as someone who as a little girl also wanted to stay invisible, who wished she could stand still and not be seen or harmed. Watching her strut into the room where she felt safe and loved as she stood tall in her power, commanding attention, reminded me that I have a choice to do the same thing. At times when I feel vulnerable or outside of my comfort zone in a public setting, I do a little "TA-DA!" in my mind.

When I host my empowerment events, I like to tell the "TA-DA" story as an invitation to people to fully show up, be present, receive; be playful and have fun. Nina's legacy continues to live on every time I share her story.

Mocha Bean

Mocha, Mocha Bean, was a feral cat I rescued. She had long, black fur and big, yellow-green eyes. As you might imagine with a feral cat, Mocha was afraid of everyone and everything. She was so afraid to be brought out into the public and would get so agitated and stressed that the foster mom stopped taking her anywhere. So, when I adopted her, I had to go the foster owner's home to meet her.

Of course, we really don't know what goes on inside a pet's head, or what experiences they have had and how they have been affected by them. Animals are sensitive to their environments, though, and Mocha was no different. It took her a long time to feel safe and to understand that she was now in a loving, caring environment. I learned patience from Mocha.

Over time I did eventually earn her trust. As she got older she became less fearful and eventually turned into a little love bug! She liked to lay on my shoulder (and she was a large cat), and to be held. You could just look at her and she would start purring, because you noticed her and she knew you would pet her. She had her favorite toy mouse that she would hunt, carry around, and play with.

She loved to drink water from the faucet, and she ate flowers. They were like catnip to her. I don't know why she did this, but I could not keep flowers around because she would bite the tops off. No flower was safe!

Mocha was never what you would call a "people" cat (like my other cat Patches), and the one person she decided she really liked was my friend Andrea, who was allergic to cats. Mocha loved her. She would go up to her a few feet away, peer at her more closely and then back away, and inch a little closer, almost as if she were challenging her. Finally Mocha would try to rub up against Andrea, take her paw and put it on her leg, like a "Gotcha!" Andrea, with her allergies, would shrink back and say, "Look, she's looking at me. Oh, she just touched me!" But Mocha would try again every time Andrea was at my house. What did she know? What was she trying to do? Maybe she sensed Andrea's discomfort and wanted to reassure her and become friends?

That is one of the mysteries of cats which make them so fascinating to me!

Mocha Bean became such a loving, positive, warm cat who loved life. But she had not been like that in her teens. Somehow, as things shifted in her mind and body, she grew–just like we can do–and became more kind and loving, and more trusting of life. She loved life and had a strong heart and spirit.

When I adopted her, I never knew whether Mocha would ever be anything but a fearful, untrusting creature. I don't know what happened to her before she came into my life, or what made her so fearful of others, but she certainly shifted into a very loving, warm cat. I was honored to love her and give her a caring, safe home, and I learned how to be patient from her.

This is what I learned from Mocha. We each move through our lives on our own journeys, making choices along the way. We don't know each other's stories, but we know that we all have them, and we don't really have to know what they are. We can choose to be patient with each other, and give each other space, respect, and gentleness.

I have also learned to choose to be with people who support me and lift me up in positive ways, who feel safe to be with and who bring out the best in me, as I do with them. When I made these kinds of choices in my early adult years, I too began to shift how I view the world and my place in it, just like Mocha Bean did.

I hope we all become braver, more living, and kind as we grow older; I hope that when someone looks at us they see peace, grace, and love. I hope our paw prints in other people's lives show kindness and love, just like Mocha Bean.

Rebecca Hall Gruyter

Rebecca Hall Gruyter is a Global Influencer, #1 International Best-Selling Author and Compiler, Publisher, Radio show Host (reaching over 1 million listeners on 7 networks), and an Empowerment leader that wants to help you reach more people. She has built multiple platforms to help experts reach more people. These platforms include: Radio, TV, books, magazines, the Speaker Talent Search, and Live Events ...Creating a powerful promotional reach of over 10 million!

Rebecca is the CEO of RHG Media Productions (which includes the RHG TV Network-with over 30 weekly programs and Publishing Arm—that has helped 200+ authors become best sellers!). She is the Owner of Your Purpose Driven Practice and the Creator of the Speaker Talent Search.

Rebecca has personally contributed to 20+ published books, multiple magazines, and has been quoted in Major Media: The Huffington Post, ABC, CBS, NBC, Fox, and Thrive Global. She now helps experts get quoted in major media too.

Today, she wants to share with you how you can be seen, be heard, and SHINE!

www.YourPurposeDrivenPractice.com
www.RHGTVNetwork.com
www.SpeakerTalentSearch.com
Rebecca@YourPurposeDrivenPractice.com

Social Media:
www.EmpoweringWomenTransformingLives (radio show)

Facebook:

www.facebook.com/rhallgruyter
www.facebook.com/pages/Rebecca-Hall-Gruyter/442052769207010
LinkedIn: www.linkedin.com/pub/rebecca-hall-gruyter/9/266/280
Twitter: www.twitter.com/Rebeccahgruyter
Instagram: RHGTVNetwork

PAW PRINTS ON MY SOUL
BY JAIMIE HARNAGEL

Animals are many things and they come in many forms. Most people probably think of them as pets (all kinds of pets...dogs, cats, birds, fish, hamsters, snakes, etc.), and believe they are there for domestication or entertainment, or something cute to cuddle. In reality, they are our friends, our family, and our confidants. They depend on us and we depend on them. To me, they are all these things, but they are also my teachers, my support system, my spirit guides, and wonderful energetic healers. Animals are divine mirrors for our souls–they show us our shadows, the things we need to resolve, and help bring our attention to what we need to work on. They are here to help us on our path to enlightenment if we can only see them for what they are.

It may seem like we choose our animals, but in reality, they choose us, coming in when we need them the most, knowing the master plan when we might not.

A relationship with an animal can awaken a part of your soul.

My story...

I have almost always been around animals. When I was young, we had an array of pets...dogs, goats, chickens, horses, geese, and peacocks. For the last twenty-five years, I have been blessed with feline energy. At one point we had five (yes, five!) cats. Still not quite sure how that happened, but as I was talking to my animal communicator (more on this topic later) at that time, she told me that they were all there to support and balance me out. Apparently I needed all five of them. Seriously?? As it turns out, she was right on the money.

My cats are my gurus. They show me how to just BE. They remind me to stay grounded. One even insists on reminding me (very loudly, I might add) that I need to sage (clear) myself or my space at certain times when something is going on. Animals make it so easy to be our authentic selves.

On death and dying...

All of my animal friends have brought something different to the table and each one of them has helped me in ways I could not have imagined. One year, I lost three of them in the course of ten months, and that was one of the roughest years of my life. At the same time, it was truly an awakening of my soul. I felt I was torn apart and then put back together. Interestingly, our youngest at four years old, passed the day after my birthday, and our oldest at seventeen, passed the day after my husband's birthday. They each gave us the gift of one more day to share and celebrate life together. Then, their time was complete.

When that veil has been lifted, and we can understand the true nature of animals as well as death, there is no going back. Your heart feels like an open wound, but at the same time, there is a deeper understanding of love and peace. I have learned that the love never dies. Our animal friends stay with us even in spirit, and you can feel them all around you. There is a deeper sense of perspective.

Another lesson I have learned is that it is not uncommon for animals to come back to the same family. We all travel in soul circles.

My Tribe

As I reflect on each animal that has come into my life, I recognize the gifts and lessons they have brought me. Each relationship was/is unique and special to me.

Simba: Unconditional Love.

Simba taught me how to savor the sweetness of life in the little moments, to pause and feel the love. As a spirit animal, hummingbirds represent the lightness of being and enjoyment of life, so to me, it is not surprising that a hummingbird stayed in the window as he transitioned. This is his sign to me now.

I first met Simba when we moved to Orlando. My kitty at that time (Rasja) was really sick and I spent a lot of time at the vet's office. While there, I saw kittens for adoption, and saw two black ones that were so perfect. I pondered getting one as a companion for Rasja, but thought, how could I separate them? After thinking about it for a week or so, I decided not to get either, as we really did not want three cats at the time (we were in temp housing). Then I had to go back to the vet (all Rasja's doing) and I saw only one kitten. I asked about the other one, and they said he had already been adopted. Of course, right then and there, I knew we were supposed to have this little one that remained. But I have to admit, as cute as he was, I did not quite gel with him until a year or so later, I think in large part because I just didn't see his light. When I finally did, I saw his huge heart.

He was a very tall cat with long legs and a long tail. He would stand on his back legs and open door handles, so much so that we finally had to get round knobs instead of the levers!

We had seventeen beautiful years together and I know he is planning on coming back around again.

<u>Nahla</u>: Strength, Courage, Grounding.

We always knew there would be a Nahla for our Simba, but it took us thirteen years to find her. And when I did, I was not even sure she was the one. When we first visited Nahla at the shelter, she looked different than I expected. She acted disinterested, and it didn't feel like we clicked. Then I realized that she did not feel good due to the load of vaccines they had given her the day before and just wanted to be left alone, but I still was not 100% sure. I called my animal communicator, who knew I was going to see this kitty at the shelter, and she confirmed it was her.

She was the mama bear...she would swat anyone that came close but she took care of everyone from a distance, even her twin soul, Simba. She would just hold the space for everyone and heal with her gentle grounding energy.

Even though she passed two years ago, she is still always present. Recently, late at night, she showed up when a customer service representative, who did not know she had passed, randomly asked about her. The next morning, a hummingbird (she shares this symbol with Simba) woke me up by consistently tapping on the glass door. What a wonderful confirmation that Nahla's spirit is always around.

Even through her passing, which I had to handle alone as my husband was out of the country, she taught me resilience and showed me that I am stronger than I think I am.

<u>Perla</u>: Comfort and Light.

She brings in a lightness. Like me, she is very sensitive to energy. She has never really played with the other cats but I watch her play with and talk to fairies. I cannot see them, but I watch her having a ball, and know what she is doing. She has fairy energy herself. When we got her, I almost named her Pixie or Tink because I felt that energy from her.

She was originally someone else's cat whom I pet sat for a few times. During one of these times she had to be rushed to the vet. The emergent issues were going to cost a considerable amount and the owner could not take them on. Unfortunately, without treatment, she was going to have to be put down so she would not suffer. I called my husband from the vet hospital and being the wonderful man that he is, he said, "Just have them take care of her and bring her home; we'll keep her." And so, she became ours. The magic of this was that she was meant to be there. At this same time, Rasja was diagnosed with cancer. I believe that he, along with our guides, engineered this so we would have her to comfort us when he left his body, which was three months later.

<u>Rasja</u>: Keeper of my soul and spiritual guide.

I cannot seem to walk this Earth without him by my side. The first time he transitioned was on Valentine's Day and my heart was shattered. I did not think I would ever recover. I couldn't understand how life could just go on as it did before. Most people would not understand, because after all, this is just a cat. Well, he wasn't and nothing is ever "just a cat or a dog".

Every living being has a purpose. Every living being has a soul.

Over time, I have learned that our relationship went much deeper than even I knew back then.

I did not know how animal communication worked or how animals came back to the same family, or that we walked in soul circles over many lifetimes. I had heard of these things, but never knew how it worked, or what to do. A friend referred me to an animal communicator who walked me through every step of the grieving process. Through the communicator, I was able to "talk" to Rasja, and our conversations gave me comfort beyond words. I also learned that he would be coming back to me, and that gave me hope.

Even with that comfort and knowing some of the details of how he would come back to us, I literally could not survive without him here physically. I got very sick and was hospitalized for three weeks. I almost died, and one day, during that time in the hospital, I felt his presence come through strongly. When I came home to recover, I was still grieving, but the doctor told me I needed to walk as much as I could, so I would walk every night. While out there, I would literally rant and rave at the Universe, insisting, no, DEMANDING! that the Universe give him back. When I did get him back (and yes, it's him!), it all became clear...that he would be back over and over again throughout my lifetime. Over the course of the years, I have come to realize that we have actually shared many lifetimes together and that he will always be by my side. There is now a deeper understanding of the role we play in each other's lives, and knowing our partnership spans many lifetimes brings a huge comfort.

He consistently shows me that I need to better manage my stress and the flow of energy in my body. We both have digestive issues, we both need a set routine, etc. In every way, he is my mirror. The minute I am anxious or out of sorts, he is yelling and trying to get my attention and get me to ground myself. When I am up late working and tired, he is yelling at me to go to bed. Really, for the most part, I get meowed (yelled) at all day long because apparently I am never doing what I am supposed to be doing!

Bodhi: Pure Joy.

Up until Bodhi, all our cats had Disney names (which is why Perla had her name instead of Pixie or Tink), with five letters and a double meaning to each one. With him, I struggled...nothing fit except Bodhi. He had so much of the Earth element in him so I named him for the Bodhi Tree. Bodhi also means awakened or enlightened, and I believe this life was all about spiritual awakening for him and me, for it was through his passing that I grew leaps and bounds in my spiritual practice, whereas he was learning freedom from the cycle of life, being free of his physical form.

He was one of several feral kitties that would come around for food when we were living in New Jersey and we decided that we would take him in. The problem was that he was "in the wild". How would I ever get to a point to actually bring him inside? I would spend several hours outside with him every evening, slowly gaining his trust, and then finally, on the eve of Hurricane Sandy (that definitely sped up my timeline!), I was able to get him in the carrier and bring him in. He battled his carrier all night and by morning he was exhausted. But we continued our courtship, and even though he had to visit the vet hospital (check-up, chipped, neutered), slowly over time, he began to trust me.

He had this BIG cat energy and these huge paws, which I loved. While he was a kitten, I always thought he would grow into them, which he did from a personality standpoint, but not physically. At the time he came in, we already had three cats, so of course, the dynamics changed. He was a wild child and brought that outdoor energy in to an otherwise calm and quiet household.

Every time I came home, he would come bounding out to see what was happening, looking for action, and I would feel this huge ball of energy coming at me. After he was gone, every time I walked into the house it was so quiet and felt completely empty, despite there still being four cats in the house. It was a horrible feeling. There was just this huge hole in the energy field and I felt his loss so keenly.

He chose to send me butterflies to help me cope with the loss. Butterflies showed up everywhere for months after his passing, and I knew it was him. Even on the day of Nahla's transition, he came to hover behind me as the vet took her outside. The vet was actually the one who noticed it right away and was amazed as well.

Each time an animal comes in or passes, it changes the dynamic and the energy in the home.

We had a mutual love affair, a special bond, and I miss his huge presence in our home.

At the same time…I'm not worried, he'll be back soon. ☺

Animal Communication

Animals understand so much more than people think they do, and they are so connected to Spirit. Anyone can communicate with animals intuitively, by sending or receiving thoughts (or images). We are all born with this capability. All you have to do is quiet the mind, and tune in, heart-to-heart with the animal. They hear most of what we think anyway.

I often think, "I d like to see them do this or that" and then, maybe within a day, I see the result. For example, when Nahla was here, I wanted to get her out more during family time in the evenings, so I just put that intention out there to her and she started showing up. The two we have now have not been best pals, but I wanted them to be able to find comfort in each other, so I imagined the two of them sitting on the couch curled up together…this took a few weeks, but it has worked out, and they have grown to trust each other in that space.

Dear Reader,

What are animals in your life saying to you? What are they bringing into your life? How are they sharing their gifts with you? Take a moment to lean in and listen, feel, and experience the magic of these powerful connections.

Feel the love.

Jaimie Harnagel

Jaimie Harnagel is a Crystal Talker, Reiki Master, Shamanic Practitioner, Animal Communicator, and Author.

While working with any healing modality, she channels her holistic practice of mind, body, and spirit into opportunities to encourage others to shine.

Jaimie co-authored "*Step Forward and Shine*" and "*Empowering you and Transforming Lives*" and was featured in RHG Magazine.

Her mission to lift up and inspire others to share their own beautiful light with the world is strongly threaded through every project she accepts.

Jaimie resides in Northern California with her husband and two furry friends who rule the roost.

jaimieharnagel.com

SHERMAN, MY VERY FIRST AND BEST FRIEND
BY REBECCA HALL GRUYTER

"How it is that animals understand things I do not know, but it is certain that they do understand. Perhaps there is a language which is not made of words and everything in the world understands it. Perhaps there is a soul hidden in everything and it can always speak, without even making a sound, to another soul." — Frances Hodgson Burnett

Sherman was my first cat, an orange and white tabby, lanky with a long tail and a soft, furry white belly. I was a young child and living trapped in a very dysfunctional, unsafe home. Then he came into my life.

Sherman was all boy, and a very confident, indoor-outdoor cat who ruled our neighborhood like a tough alley cat. He would get into fights—and win, no matter if it was with another cat or a large dog! He did not really like anyone in the family but me.

He was a difficult cat for the family because he was not nice to them. If you asked my brother, he'd say, "That cat just peed on everything! And he scratched and laid on my pillow and made me sick." My brother was allergic to cats, so that is what he remembers.

I remember Sherman differently. To me he was gentle; he took care of me, and he loved me unconditionally. Every night he would lay beside me in bed, like a person, with his head up on the pillow and his body tucked in. He would stay there until I fell asleep. He was my friend and protector, keeping away the scary things at night so I could fall asleep.

Sherman could never know what a gift he was to me, or maybe he did. In my early years, I was living in an abusive home. I spent my days in fear, learning to stay below the radar, knowing that it was not safe to be seen or heard. Sherman was the friend I could count on, who loved me, and was soft and safe, without judgment. It was him and me against the world, and he was always on my side.

He was kind to my friends too, I guess because he knew they loved me. One of them even wrote a poem about him—an ode to Sherman, about how beautiful he was sitting in the sun. He let us all hug him, and when I called him he would come running. It was a very special connection.

So, Sherman taught me a lot about love, and helped me to feel love when I did not feel loved by many others. This was very important at that time in my life, when my environment was so unsafe, hostile, and dangerous. He was my golden guardian and my friend.

Even though he was this tough, rough and tumble cat in the neighborhood, Sherman let me do anything—even dress him up! I would put him in a doll stroller, paws and belly up, dressed up in doll clothes with a little hat, and I pushed him around the neighborhood like he was my baby. He took it like a good sport, every time.

As I think about it now, it makes me laugh. There he was, in a hat and dress, being pushed in a stroller past all the people, dogs, and cats he had been bullying. What a buzz that must have caused!

As Frances Hodgson Burnett so beautifully says, how do animals understand us and know us so well? Sherman and I definitely had a common language, spoken through the soul. He had an uncanny way of knowing when I needed him to cuddle up, to be playful, to keep me company, and to guard me from the dark of night. His unconditional love for me carried me through a difficult time in my life, and continues to supports me today.

Author and biologist Rupert Sheldrake explains it this way: "When a [pet] is strongly bonded to its owner, this bond persists even when the owner is far away and is, I think, the basis of telepathic communication. I see telepathy as a normal, not paranormal, means of communication between members of animal groups." Have you found that to be true of the animals in your life? I know it has been true for me.

Darla and Alfie

What have I learned from Sherman? I learned how important it is for someone to be there for you in your time of need. That was how siblings Darla and Alfie entered our lives.

My neighbor came to us with a dilemma. She was trying to decide what to do with these cats that had been thrust upon her by a family who did not want them—they had been shuttled around and landed with my neighbor. She asked my husband, Andrew, if we would take them in, and he said, "Well, let me talk to Rebecca," feeling hesitation because they were elderly. We thought they were eight, but they turned out to be much older. We decided we would still take them into our home and provide the love and care needed to give them a forever home.

I have had special needs cats in my life, and have experience rescuing them, and helping them with their fears or illnesses, finding the connection and care. It felt normal to me. To me, animals are family and you do not always get to choose how your family comes. We are responsible for our family, not just when it is convenient or easy. Sherman, Darla, Alfie—none of the pets in my life had a choice for who their family was! So, that is how I felt about taking in Darla and Alfie, and I was so happy when Andrew came up with the solution for them, as he was not used to having cats in his life like I was.

So, twenty-one teeth extractions, extreme fearfulness, arthritis, and—for Darla, a permanent furless ring around her neck from a collar that had been too tight and never taken off—later, they are still in our lives today, just beautiful cats who are such cuddle bugs with big personalities! I think of how difficult it must have been for them to be around people who did not connect with them, to be turned away, passed from home to home. Yet they were still willing to love and be loved, and I am honored that we are the ones that get to connect with them now. I also feel in some way that I am honoring Sherman, grateful for all he meant to me when I needed unconditional love and connection.

From sharing my life with these beautiful animals, I have also learned about loving fellow humans. We all have our stories, perhaps our "special needs." There are choices in our lives that we did not get to make, whether related to our background, dysfunctional family, accidents that occur to us or loved ones, financial reversals, or difficult losses and deaths. But even the choices we do not get to make can be stepping stones on the path that leads us to our purpose and joy. We can choose care and love, to love and be loved.

Despite everything that may happen TO us in our lives, we do have at least one choice that is ours to make. We can still be empowered and choose our response to those things that happen. All of the things that happen to us can become the fuel that propels us forward. We can still find solutions to deal with the difficulties. We can still feel gratitude for all that we do have and will create for ourselves. We can still choose love.

Source:**https://fractalenlightenment.com/36761/life/ the-telepathic-connection-between-animals-and-humans**

Rebecca Hall Gruyter

Rebecca Hall Gruyter is a Global Influencer, #1 International Best-Selling Author and Compiler, Publisher, Radio Show Host (reaching over 1 million listeners on 7 networks), and an Empowerment Leader that wants to help you reach more people. She has built multiple platforms to help experts reach more people. These platforms include: Radio, TV, books, magazines, the Speaker Talent Search, and Live Events–creating a powerful promotional reach of over 10 million!

Rebecca is the CEO of RHG Media Productions (which includes the RHG TV Network-with over 30 weekly programs and Publishing Arm—that has helped 200+ authors become best sellers! She is the owner of Your Purpose Driven Practice and the creator of the Speaker Talent Search.

Rebecca has personally contributed to 20+ published books, multiple magazines, and has been quoted in Major Media: The Huffington Post,

ABC, CBS, NBC, Fox, and Thrive Global. And now helps Experts get quoted in major media too.

Today, she wants to share with you: How you too, can be seen, be heard and SHINE!

www.YourPurposeDrivenPractice.com
www.RHGTVNetwork.com
www.SpeakerTalentSearch.com
Rebecca@YourPurposeDrivenPractice.com

Social Media:
www.EmpoweringWomenTransformingLives (radio show)

Facebook:
www.facebook.com/rhallgruyter
www.facebook.com/pages/Rebecca-Hall-Gruyter/442052769207010
LinkedIn: **www.linkedin.com/pub/rebecca-hall-gruyter/9/266/280**
Twitter: **www.twitter.com/Rebeccahgruyter**
Instagram: RHGTVNetwork

SECTION 3:

Animal Legacy Friends & Family

ANIMAL SPIRIT GUIDES
BY MICHELLE PETICOLAS, PH.D.

The word *animal* comes from the Latin *anima* meaning *breath* or *soul*. There was a time when humans recognized the spiritual nature of the land and its inhabitants. This recognition is something many humans have lost in this modern world of commerce and consumerism.

When we allow them, animals can connect us to our spiritual being.

The purring cat draws us into a meditative state. Dogs lead us into nature and play. If we take the time to observe, wild animals will pull us more deeply into the spirit of the natural world.

Some animals, like crows or owls, have been thought to herald a death. Others seem to assist deceased loved ones in communicating with us from beyond.

Our own inner wisdom may speak to us in animal symbols through our dreams or life encounters. And of course, animals can guide us with their own innate animal wisdom.

I have been privileged with animal guidance throughout my life dating all the way back to my childhood before my earliest memories.

A Herd of White Horses

Born into a family already occupied by two elder siblings, I often worried about belonging and being wanted. I never bonded with my mom. I briefly bonded with my Dad, who, unfortunately, was transferred to Japan when I was only two. I felt abandoned and betrayed. Although we were reunited several months later, our close relationship never fully resumed.

At that time my middle sister had become my closest connection. We played together for hours, giggling and making up games and stories. When she turned five, and began school, I felt alone again.

According to my mother, and I have no memory of this, I began sharing a story about a herd of white horses that watched over me. I ran with them, rode on their backs, and flew in the air. They were my constant companions.

My mother was so captivated by this story that she rendered it in oils. Two white figures on a dark blue canvas observe each other under a crescent moon, a young girl in ballet costume and a prancing white horse.

I do not know how long the horses stayed with me, but one day, as the story goes, the horses flew up into the night sky and became stars where they could watch over me forever.

Young children, especially lonely young children, are known to tell stories about "imaginary friends." An imaginary friend is an invisible playmate who enables a child to feel loved, valued, and less alone.

In recalling this story of the horses, I found myself wondering whether these friends were really *imaginary*. If one believes in other worldly intervention and guidance, it is not so difficult to believe that young children may actually be seeing angelic guardians in child-friendly forms.

Through socialization and adaption to the dominant culture, this childhood connection may be lost. But, it need not be lost forever. Even now, we may learn to access the wisdom of our otherworldly guides through meditation and our animal connections.

I love that my mother preserved the story of my magical horse herd in her painting and that, when I was old enough, she shared it with me. I should not be surprised that she did this. Born under the mystical astrology sign of Pieces, my mother had esoteric leanings, which she annually demonstrated at our New Year's divination ritual with the I Ching book of Changes. It was she who gave me my very first Tarot deck, which was so instrumental in setting me on a spiritual path.

I believe she knew something special had happened to me with those horses and rendered it on canvas so that I might never forget. I never have.

Hobji the Purple Dinosaur

When I was about ten years old, another significant animal came into my life: Hobji (pronounced Hob-jah-eye), a purple dinosaur. My own creation, Hobji was a comical version of the Tyrannosaurus Rex.

Hobji stood upright, and had a mouth full of sharp teeth and a massive bulk. Hobji could take care of himself. It was a talent I needed to acquire in order to not be over-shadowed by my siblings.

If you laughed at Hobji, which you might when he walked his armadillo watchdog, he would sit on you and squash you or beat you into a snarl.

Through the illustrations that flowed from my pencil, Hobji taught me how to hold my own. He showed me how to be powerful, and to stand up for myself and protect my feelings with sharp humor and wit. The armadillo watched over my tender heart.

Although my older sisters were much better artists than I was, Hobji gave me an edge. He was totally unique and my mother loved him. Years later when she was trying her hand at greeting cards, she asked if she could use him. I said yes, but of course, her Hobji was never mine.

In spite of being grumpy and a little intimidating, Hobji had a lot of friends—mouse, rabbit, frog, snake (who traveled by skateboard) and, of course, the armadillo watchdog.

For a while, I created a comic strip, which appeared in a homemade newspaper written and edited by my sister and me. We managed to put out two editions before the challenge of columns alignment on a play typewriter defeated us.

Eventually, school and other interests reduced my cartooning to a trickle. Hobji and his friends made infrequent appearances in birthday cards and gift tags.

They staged a big comeback when I began my career as a grief and loss coach. First, they appeared in my mini-book, *Essentials for Grieving Well.* Then they showed up in a PowerPoint presentation on caregiving. More recently they have clarified my messages on Facebook, Instagram, Pinterest, and in my blogs.

Rabbit, rat, frog, and Hobji help wake people up to important issues of life, such as loss, aging, caregiving, and death. They do this with unguarded expressions and disarming humor. Loss and change are easier to appreciate when accompanied with laughter.

Hobji is kinder now then he was when I was a child, more compassionate and loving. No longer afraid of appearing silly or weak, he reveals how to be courageous and vulnerable at the same time. When he emerges from my pencil, he mirrors my soul. The armadillo watchdog has disappeared, as my heart has lost much of its armor.

Lao-Tzu, the Nurturer

Not all of my animal guides have been imaginary. Lao-Tzu, a long-haired Siamese cat, was flesh and blood.

Lao-Tzu is the name of a 6th century BC Chinese philosopher, who is traditionally regarded as the founder of Taoism. He is the author of the Tao-te-Ching, its most sacred scripture.

In the late seventies, not long after losing my first real job as a Sociology instructor, I landed a position with my husband as house parents for a group home in Las Vegas, Nevada.

The group home consisted of five court-placed teenage girls between the ages of thirteen and eighteen. The treatment plan was to immerse these at-risk youths in a structured and stable home environment where they could develop confidence and independence through instruction and corrective intervention by the *teaching* house parents.

Based on Behavioral Theory, the group home program used a system of rewards and punishments in the form of points that motivated desired behavior. The points could be exchanged for privileges, e.g. watching TV, going to the movies, special time with the house parents, etc. Loss of points would lead to loss of privileges.

There are some very excellent aspects to the behavioral approach, i.e. focusing on changeable behavior rather than emotions and the systematic practice of teaching skills and encouraging incremental successes. I use aspects of this methodology in my own coaching, although without a point system.

Some of the girls in our program had engaged in delinquent behavior, while others simply came from dysfunctional homes. Learning how to help them entailed a steep learning curve.

I could see that the girls' misbehaviors, in many cases, could be traced to lack of affection and attention from their busy or overwhelmed parents. Misbehavior, although it might not obtain affection, usually got attention, and that was often better than nothing.

I knew first-hand the emotional pain that is triggered by lack of attention from my own childhood. Unlike these girls, however, my attention seeking was more socially acceptable, i.e. good grades and creativity. They could do that too, when encouraged in that direction.

It was clear that these girls needed attention and regard, but I did not know how to connect with them. I had learned few nurturing skills in my childhood.

I decided that the way to develop these skills was to get a kitten.

My husband and I drove to the local animal shelter to check out the options. Almost at once, a young Siamese cat caught my attention. He was no kitten! Yet, I could not take my eyes off him. He purred, he spoke to me, and he drew me in. No other animal existed. I knew we were meant for each other, and I took him home.

It is amazing how the universe responds to our intentions when we are clear and heart-felt.

The first thing I noticed was that Lao-Tzu was mine. He gave his attention to no one but me. This was a new experience! When I was a child, all the cats bonded with my mom. She was, after all, the one who fed them. This connection with Lao-Tzu, however, was different. No matter who fed him, this cat knew we had a soul contract.

A short time after Lao-Tzu moved in, we decided to give him a companion and brought home a long-haired female Siamese kitten. She was tiny, confused, and clearly missing her mom. Lao-Tzu gave me my first lesson in nurturing by taking her under his wing. He washed her, slept with her, and even allowed her to pretend-nurse on his belly.

I was surprised by this behavior. If a tomcat could be nurturing, I figured, so could I.

My ability to express real affection for the girls improved. They actually began to like me and seek my attention. This proved to be one of the most powerful motivators and became one of our rewards. Connection, however, is a two-way street, and fraught with peril when you do not set boundaries. We made mistakes in this regard and lost our position after barely a year. Working 24/7 probably did not help the situation.

Lao-Tzu and the kitten Lilly came with us to our next group home position, which was in Ft. Defiance, Arizona on the Navajo reservation. Hoogan Joobaai (Ho-gon Joe-bye-eee), the name of the home, means *house of care*. In this home we cared for six emotionally challenged Navajo youth between the ages of thirteen and eighteen, both boys and girls.

A great improvement over our first group home job, this position actually gave us three days off per week and an alternate couple to work with. Our off-duty residence was across the drive from the group home and as small as a shoebox. But to us, it seemed liked paradise.

Our cats adjusted quite readily to the twice-weekly shift in location, especially after we installed a cat door. Six months later, the first batch of kittens arrived. Once more, Lao-Tzu demonstrated his nurturing skills. After the kittens were born, he kissed the mom and checked out each kitten.

Later, when the kittens became older and Lilly was tired of motherhood, Lao-Tzu took over by letting them sleep with him.

Another thing Lao-Tzu did that was surprising was how he waited for me by the front door whenever I returned from a trip. He would not move until I acknowledged him. My husband initially alerted me to this unusual behavior with, "Your cat is waiting for you!" Eventually, I began to notice on my own. His insistence on connection shifted my awareness of others. He taught me to pause and pay attention, which serves me well as a healer.

One day, after about three years of living on the Navajo Reservation, Lao-Tzu failed to return. Many things could have happened to him–coyotes, dogs, even bears. We never found out. He simply vanished. I like to think he had finished his contract with me and moved on to his next assignment.

Animal Lessons

The key to receiving animal guidance is receptivity. When we are open and aware, animals can teach us many things about ourselves and help us grow. My animal guides taught me to love myself, to love others, and to have enough courage to step out of limiting beliefs about myself. Animals continue to guide me even now, mostly through dreams and my drawings. I find them everywhere—a bluebird, a turkey, a friendly cat greeting me on the sidewalk, Hobji climbing out of the La Brea Tar Pit. All you need to do is stop and listen. Notice what feelings come up. There is always a message. What are animals in your life sharing with you?

Dr. Michelle Peticolas

Dr. Michelle Peticolas is a best-selling author, national speaker, life coach and artist. She empowers leaders and change-makers to overcome their fears and limiting beliefs in order to fully step into their authentic power and make a difference in this world.

She has a Ph.D. in Sociology and over eighteen years of experience coaching people through major life challenges. Drawing from recent work in neuropsychology, evolutionary biology, and psychosomatics, and thirty-five years of spiritual practice, Dr. Peticolas has developed powerful tools that promote body intelligence and mental mastery.

The daughter of a successful toy designer, Michelle has been drawing animal characters since the age of eleven. These delightful illustrations are used in her blogs and books to ease our resistance to the challenges and lessons of loss, change, death, and grief. Hobji, a purple dinosaur who is the main character in her storyline, reflects and reveals many of the landmarks and turning points of Michelle's own life journey.

Michelle leads workshops for universities, hospitals, and professional organizations, including The Commonwealth Club of San Francisco. Her work appeals to diverse audiences interested in enhancing and developing their skills and effectiveness in managing and coping with social change. Her unique programs like **From Loss to Success in Love, Health and Wealth** and No Regret Now are designed for professional women to heal emotional wounds and traumas so they can stand in their power and fulfill their mission.

She is a featured author in the best-selling anthology *Breaking Barriers*, and the recently released international best-seller, *Step Into Your Brilliance*.

Email: mp@secretsoflifeanddeath.com
Phone: 510-859-4145
Website: **https://www.secretsoflifeanddeath.com**
https://www.facebook.com/secretsoflifeanddeath
https://www.linkedin.com/in/michellepeticolas/
https://twitter.com/secretsofnow
https://www.youtube.com/channel/UCpLeJ9ZBjETCqcmVkRPBtCg
https://www.pinterest.com/secretsofdeath/
https://instagram.com/michellepeticolas

SQUIRRELS AND SHREWS AND CROWS, OH MY!
BY REBECCA HALL GRUYTER

For as long as I can remember, I have loved animals–all creatures, great and small. I always felt a special connection with them.

As a young child I loved playing outdoors, and would I bring garter snakes, snails, and other little creatures into the house. They were my playmates. When I was around seven years old I gathered some caterpillars to be in my circus; I was convinced that I had taught one to do some tricks! Hey, maybe it was true. I was pretty sure at the time. I was always gentle with these creatures, and when we were finished "playing" I would release them back to their homes unharmed.

I touched and fed wild animals like squirrels and rabbits, and they would interact with me. I have touched deer that have come up to me. I was always capturing frogs, making pets out of them. Once I caught two frogs mating, so I got to raise a whole family from tadpoles and we released them back into the wild.

There was no fear, and I was never bitten.

This whole thing really terrified my mom and my Grandma Ives, of course, because these were "diseased animals" and they were afraid I would be bitten and get rabies.

When I was seven years old, I was at my Grandma Ives' house one day. I was playing outdoors with my cat Sherman, who traveled to Grandma's with us, when suddenly a little creature ran onto my lap. I started petting the poor little thing and shooed Sherman away so he would not grab it (I learned later that the animal was a shrew). It seemed to know everything was okay, and stayed in my lap while I continued to pet it. I was sure it was thanking me. My Grandma approached, and seeing the creature on my lap, screamed, "Get that off you!" I looked up in shock, but gently set the shrew down on the ground and it scurried off.

I did not understand Grandma Ives' reaction at all. Now I know now she was just being protective, but to me, it was just a poor little creature and I was protecting it from Sherman. I was so surprised by her reaction because somehow inside me I just knew it could trust me and I could trust it, that I could pet it just like I would a cat or a horse.

To this day I find it interesting that we are taught to be afraid of animals like mice, and to hate or keep away from animals because we are supposed to assume they are dangerous or diseased. I believed as a child that animals are empathic like I am, and I continue to believe that as an adult.

How special is the wonderment of children when we do not have any fear and treat all beings the same way, without judgment!

In what ways do you see wondrous things in your life?

Even as an adult, I like to look for wonder in my life, to see the magic that might present itself to me at any moment. Here is a powerful exercise to invite wonderment and magic in, by setting your expectations for it. When you are about to enter a new situation or go to an event, check in with yourself by asking:

"What is it that I need to know or have [in this situation or at this event]?"

"What will encourage me, equip me, and empower me to bring in my magic?"

"*What is it that I'm willing to receive in this experience I am about to have?*"

Then open yourself up to connect with the answers. You may find wonder in the most unexpected places!

We are empowered with the choice to hold things in our lives in wonder and awe, no matter what other people tell us. We can make the decisions for ourselves what we will trust and how we will treat each other. We can choose the lens through which we see our world. I learned this from my Grandma Quinn who was an amazing observer of animals and the natural world.

Those rascal crows

My Grandma Quinn lived in Washington in a mobile home on a beautiful piece of land in the forest. Even at an advanced age and after multiple strokes, she lived on her own among the trees and beauty, because she loved so much. She loved life. She loved science and learning new things, and would spend hours just observing what was around her.

One of the things she noticed year after year were the "rascal crows" as she called them. She would call me to tell me the crows were drunk again from eating all the cherries from the tree near her house.

She described how they would trip over each other, stagger around crookedly, and sometimes even block the road so cars could not get by. "These rascally crows are misbehaving. They're drunk!" I could hear their cackling in the background while she was talking about them.

After this same conversation happened for a few years, finally I decided to do some research on crows. Crows are those creatures we see every day, big and black and noisy. But we do not pay attention to them, except that they are often depicted as dark or evil. Well, I learned some interesting things about crows. They form lifelong partnerships, and stay together as a cluster or family. They are so verbose because they are communicating with each other, maybe like your family or mine around the dinner table! They are just a loud, rambunctious animal, hanging out in their families. I began to see them differently.

But do they get drunk?

Well, Grandma has since passed away, and now there is a cherry tree in front of our property and one near my office. The crows come every year and, yes, they eat the cherries (fermented berries will cause birds to get drunk), and stumble around, loud and fighting and having a great time. Every time I see them I can hear my Grandma sharing her wonder, observation and appreciation of those "rascal crows."

It just always lifts my spirit and makes me smile.

And then there were the squirrels

Grandma Quinn also once shared a story with me in a phone conversation. Her neighbors were having a party. It had gotten pretty noisy as time went on, and she went outside to see what was going on. As she sat in front of her house, she told me, "Rebecca, some squirrels got on the tree near the road, and threw pinecones down on the parked cars. It was like they liked the sound it made." The squirrels would stop and listen to the sound, and chatter away, talking amongst themselves, then start again. More and more squirrels were joining, and they dropped more pinecones, sometimes pelting several at a time.

By the time the partiers came out to go home, Grandma said she could hear them yelling and chattering (not unlike the squirrels) something about their cars. She realized that they found dents all over them! There were multiple cars that ended up being affected, as if they had been near a golfing range getting bonked by stray golf balls. She told me, "They came over and asked me if I knew what happened, and I explained it was the squirrels. I don't think they believed me." I wonder if the police or the insurance companies believed her either.

And why not? Why couldn't that have happened? It's just that she paid attention. I just love how Grandma Quinn looked out into the world with such clear yet wondering eyes, observing the animals around her with great curiosity, open to receiving the joy they brought.

It was a special gift for me, to affirm my own wonderment about animals and to remind me how compassionate I am for them.

There are many studies today that show the remarkable characteristics of animals. Like the crows, some develop a family life and language, and stay together in lifelong relationships. We know that many creatures, from bees to dolphins, share a special language that help them in their lives together. We know that animals experience emotions and feel grief. Studies have shown that chimpanzees, elephants, and magpies actually hold "funerals," vigils or social rituals, to mourn the life of one of their own.

As we think about the animals in our lives, we know them well. We know their personalities, each different and wonderful in their own way. For me, the lesson is to observe like Grandma Quinn did, curiously, lovingly, and without judgment. What else is out there waiting to be noticed or discovered when we pause and listen for it?

Of course we can do this not only with our pets but with all animals, and with other people. We can take purposeful time to observe and be curious, and to notice what someone might have to teach us, or what joy or new experience they might have for us. What can I do to touch the lives of others as they richly touch and bless mine?

We are all God's creatures, and we can love them all.

Rebecca Hall Gruyter

Rebecca Hall Gruyter is a Global Influencer, #1 International Best-Selling Author and Compiler, Publisher, Radio Show Host (reaching over 1 million listeners on 7 networks), and an Empowerment Leader that wants to help you reach more people. She has built multiple platforms to help experts reach more people. These platforms include: Radio, TV, books, magazines, the Speaker Talent Search, and Live Events, creating a powerful promotional reach of over 10 million!

Rebecca is the CEO of RHG Media Productions (which includes the RHG TV Network-with over 30 weekly programs and Publishing Arm that has helped 200+ authors become best sellers!) She is the owner of Your Purpose Driven Practice and the creator of the Speaker Talent Search.

Rebecca has personally contributed to 20+ published books, multiple magazines, and has been quoted in Major Media: The Huffington Post, ABC, CBS, NBC, Fox, and Thrive Global. And now helps experts get quoted in major media too.

Today, she wants to share with you: How you too, can be seen, be heard and SHINE!

www.YourPurposeDrivenPractice.com
www.RHGTVNetwork.com
www.SpeakerTalentSearch.com
Rebecca@YourPurposeDrivenPractice.com

Social Media:
www.EmpoweringWomenTransformingLives (radio show)

Facebook:
www.facebook.com/rhallgruyter
www.facebook.com/pages/Rebecca-Hall-Gruyter/442052769207010
LinkedIn: **www.linkedin.com/pub/rebecca-hall-gruyter/9/266/280**
Twitter: **www.twitter.com/Rebeccahgruyter**
Instagram: RHGTVNetwork

DOLPHINS! ADVENTURES
IN TRANSFORMATION AND HEALING
BY RAYNA LUMBARD, LMFT

I am so excited to share my experiences with amazing wild ocean dolphins and those living in facilities. My introduction to dolphins was through the 1960s TV show Flipper, about a very smart and entertaining dolphin that saved or helped his co-starring children save someone from danger. It was easy for children, adolescents, and even some grownups that are naturally full of wonder, laughter and love to relate to and develop an emotional connection to this smart, magical dolphin hero. You may be curious about what is so special and magical about dolphins, members of the group of mammals known as cetaceans.

Since the late 1990s there have been more and more opportunities to communicate and swim with dolphins, both in the wild and in captivity. You may be wondering why connecting with the dolphins is such a sought-after experience. Remember how you felt after seeing them entertaining audiences, at an aquarium or even at the Mirage Hotel in Las Vegas? Just ask people who will pay $200 or more to connect with these amazing creatures!

Dolphins are spiritual teachers assisting humanity in opening their hearts and elevating their consciousness. Being in somewhat close physical contact with them and even thinking about them transports many people out of their usual third or fourth dimensional worlds of ego-driven negative, dark energy forces and polarities, like right/wrong and good/bad. Dolphins create energy fields that invite us to experience a higher vibration or spiritual plane, the fifth dimension of higher wisdom, of pure light where true unconditional love, joy, and compassion replace blame, hurt, judgment, and violence. They remind us that living with fear is a choice that dissolves in this higher energy the more we become aware of what positive, magical beings we humans truly are. When I feel their sonar, uplifting energy, and playfulness, I connect with my own higher self and playful nature that is intuitive and peacefully powerful.

Dolphins live in pod communities and love to be with humans in touch with their own loving energy. Proud dolphin moms in the wild often show you their babies and give special attention to pregnant women. It is not unusual to feel a deep sense of peace, love, joy, and oneness with everyone and everything after connecting with dolphins. Many people experience a healing of mind, body, emotions, relationships, finances, and spirit to manifest their dreams! I highly recommend spending time with these awesome cetaceans.

I began my spiritual dolphin journey after receiving transmissions from the dolphin realm in 1997 by reading Ashleea Nielson's book *Dolphin Tribe* and listening to her dolphin meditations. Reading about dolphin behavior and meditating with dolphin sounds attuned me to higher frequencies. I was initiated into the Dolphin Tribe, and it has been a love affair ever since. In 2003 I swam with my first dolphin named Khyber in Bermuda through Dolphin Quest. Dancing with him and kissing him was such a blissful experience! The playful wild dolphins in Hawaii communicated with me telepathically, showing our group a new transformed paradigm for living in bliss.

As I opened my heart and breathed into my soul, I began to channel dolphin energy, healing my own personal health and relationship issues. Then I was ready to share my gifts with various transformational groups including Unconditional Awakening Journeys with Dr. Laurie Moore. I facilitated individual and group sessions with her on the Big Island in 2005 and 2006. This experience awakened group consciousness and opened hearts to more loving and joyful lives. The dolphins' messages of deep faith and transformational growth resulted in our "podners" being happier, healthier, and more successful in their everyday lives. Being a dolphin ambassador, whisperer, and healer is a precious gift I will share forever.

Since then I have presented many talks, workshops, and playshops like "Connecting and Healing Energetically with the Dolphins". I love sharing my own adventures with dolphins and whales from being in a multitude of retreats. I especially love channeling dolphin healing energy and their sounds for individuals and groups. My first trip to the Big Island of Hawaii in January 2004 on a dolphin yoga retreat was one of the highlights of my life. Snorkeling in Kealakekua Bay with the wild spinner dolphins elevated my being into higher dimensions of light and love energy. Who wouldn't want to spend quality time with our fun, playful cousins of the sea? Many people these days have connected with and swam in bays, lakes and rivers with dolphins in many locations all over the world. We have shared amazing stories of dolphins rescuing people from harm or death, being birth coaches for happy moms, assisting mentally and physically disabled people, and giving many gifts to humanity. Some of us are blessed to channel their healing sounds, embodying their healing energy, sonar, and songs. As a healing facilitator I heard the "call," dedicating my life to serving humanity on the highest level possible. Thank you dolphins for initiating me into the Dolphin Tribe in 1997, the beginning of my Dolphin Healing Adventures.

In 2008 I was guided to join Humanity Unites Brilliance as an Archangel supported by Trish Regan and Doug Hackett from Dolphin\Spirit of Hawaii. My personal and planetary mission became clearer by attending HUB's *Awakening Your Brilliance and Actioning Your Brilliance* events in California. I gave a special presentation, *Healing Energetically with the Dolphins*, along with other Archangels shortly after the HUB events as part of Dolphin\Spirit of Hawaii's five-day *Dolphins, Joy, and Brilliance Retreat*. All of the facilitators and participants were ready to dive into their souls to manifest deep transformations in our lives. This special retreat included three swims with the dolphins and energy and sound healing. Doug and Trish included their powerful Quantum Manifestation processes, and deep soul sharing brought out our higher gifts and talents to shift us into new dimensions of being. Trish and Doug are master facilitators that brought our "pod" closer together as we connected with the magical cetaceans. Thank you Trish and Doug for leaving your comfortable lives in California to take the plunge into unchartered waters with the dolphins and whales back in 1994.

I was not planning a trip in early 2009, but I found myself in a lot of pain preparing our taxes. Fortunately I had a session with a powerful Hawaiian healer on April 14, just in time. To my surprise, the dolphins called me to come to Hawaii for my birthday, May 20th. I called Trish Regan from Dolphin\Spirit of Hawaii and discovered their retreat was coming up in just two weeks! I was able to manifest attending their dolphin retreat in a heartbeat, finding a reasonable airline ticket. I was off to Hawaii, again! Trish and Doug's dolphin retreat, Ascension Dynamics, felt like home. My good friend Diana Bluer met me there. We totally immersed ourselves in the experience of a lifetime. We created a group intention and a special theme at the beginning of the retreat to accelerate the manifestation of our soul's ascension. We surrendered to our spiritual power and unconditional loving expansion to allow us to magnetize the spirit of oneness within us to manifest our soul's divine purpose. Our group soul's purpose was to live heaven on earth. Thank you dolphins for having such a divine "porpoise" for us!

My Dolphin\Spirit of Hawaii group (pod) included my friend Diana, a new friend from Switzerland, and of course Trish, Doug, and the dolphins lighting our way. We spent four mornings on several different boats with lots of opportunities to get in the water. We loved swimming and connecting energetically with the dolphins! This raised our vibration the more we swam and shared our awesome experiences in our group. The dolphins knew telepathically what we were thinking and feeling. They used their sonar to work with our emotional blocks. We asked for messages and received healings. One of the alpha males loudly focused his sonar in bullet fashion to help me release negative thoughts, putting a wide, joyful smile on my face, looking just like my new dolphin friend. I also let dolphin bubbles pop on my third eye and heart with special encoded loving messages for me. Eye gazing and parallel swimming with a dolphin is soul connecting at the highest level. The vibrational wave of love I received with this message was, "You are my beloved."

On one of our boat trips I had an amazing experience. When the captain stopped to allow us to glide into the water for yet another swim that day, my guidance said, "Rest up, the dolphins aren't going to be physically close to you this time." Then I felt a nudge to go in the water anyway to see what would happen. As I swam "outside," toward the ocean side of the boat, I saw a huge half rainbow in front of me. I love rainbows and felt very blessed to see even one half of one. Then the captain directed us to swim toward shore, "inside," where I saw the other half of the rainbow. I suddenly realized that no one else was having this experience. I asked the dolphins what this meant. I heard, "Have faith, we are always with you, blessing you." I felt a surge of power and knew that I will move here someday. I did not understand the whole message until that night when Trish channeled messages from St. Germaine. She said that there was a glitch in the timing to move here, that is why the rainbow was in two sections. I looked for real estate and found one condo I fell in love with, but it was not for my highest good to commit so much money, time, and energy into renting a place out in between visits. We continued to focus on the dolphins supporting our highest intentions to manifest our lives through our playful experiences this week. It was exhilarating! When I came back I could tap into feeling the dolphins any time I chose to, and so can you! My experiences led me to facilitate my own Dolphin Healing Adventure Retreat in Hawaii in 2016. I was inspired to write this poem after my retreat on the Big Island after connecting with my dolphin friends for almost twenty years.

Abundant Blessings from the Dolphins!

Ocean Ballerinas, Gentle and Kind,
Playful Acrobats, Enlighten our Minds.
Spinning, Twirling, Gliding Freely,
Opening our Hearts, Loving our Being.
Joyful, Blissful, Magical, and Fun,
Deepen Our Connection with the One.
Guide Our Brilliance with Grace so Bright,
Dancing Dolphins, Bless Our Healing Light

For many years now, the National Oceanic and Atmospheric Administration (NOAA) has been threatening to enact "The 50 Yard Rule" which means swimmers and boats cannot be within 50 yards of the dolphins. Of course, that would essentially stop dolphin swimming in Hawaii. They had more meetings in Hawaii in the spring of 2019, and it seemed like they were open to compromises like time closures of the bays or restricting certain areas in the bays, but more recent articles indicate that they most likely will just go ahead and write the 50 Yard Law. Of course, boat venders, dolphin retreat facilitators and the general public do not know for sure if this law will be enacted and enforced by the end of 2019. We know in our heart of hearts that in general dolphins are not being harassed by people and boats in Hawaii. They are very intelligent and take charge of doing what they need/want to do. I have come to believe that dolphins, as advanced spiritual beings, are curious about people and are living their soul purpose to enlighten and provide healing for humans and other life forms.

I am continually inspired to connect with dolphins in any way I can. While co-organizing the Cetacean Summit in Hawaii in 2014, I had the pleasure of meeting many cetacean experts and healing facilitators from all over the world. I learned even more about the dolphins' special qualities of the Higher Self that are assisting humanity in many ways. Dolphins share unconditional love and compassion, a playful, light-hearted nature, and express joyful, heart-connecting bliss. It is a given that dolphins are not only very intelligent, but also telepathic, using intuitive guidance to access higher truth. Being in their presence and energy reminds us that we, too, can create heaven on Earth and manifest the world of our dreams!

Dolphins invite you to get in touch with a specific dream or dreams for a happier, healthier, more joyful and abundant life. Then through meditation or journaling, send your intentional thoughts into the Universe with enthusiasm and passion. Keep moving forward on your path by making positive decisions that lead to choosing the right actions. Have faith that you are manifesting your dreams or even better ones that are for your highest good. Release fears that may sabotage you and trust with all your heart that your dreams are on their way and already manifested. Live authentically by being grounded in your own loving self, then connect and empower others.

Together with the dolphins' help we will catapult our species out of the destruction we have created, to a more harmonious, compassionate, magical, and blissful state of authentic Being to meet new challenges facing humanity. *Are you ready to meet "the call" to truly live your own paradise with mastery and grace?* If you say, "Yes," I encourage you to spend some time with dolphins face to face, through books, and through your own meditations.

Rayna Lumbard, LMFT

Rayna Lumbard, MA, Licensed Marriage and Family Therapist, Psychospiritual Energy/Sound Healer, and Master Hypnotherapist. Through InnerSuccess Transformations, she inspires and supports you to Transform Your Life for GOOD! Experience her powerful breakthrough technologies, "Inner Wisdom Healing Journey" and "Higher Light Connections."

She is the author of numerous publications including "Empowering Your Divine Life Purpose," the lead chapter in **Authentic Alignment.**

Rayna has been fascinated with dolphins and channeling their healing energy since 1997. She especially loves ocean swimming close to them on the Big Island of Hawaii. In her presentations, Rayna shares her healing adventures with the cetaceans, and invites you to explore interspecies communication, sharing how to expand your playful connections by tapping into dolphin love, joy, abundance, and bliss through the media, in person groups, or private healing sessions.

Are you ready to...

Connect with your higher self and spiritual guidance from the dolphins to open your intuition and telepathic channels?

Raise your vibration by receiving healing light energy and profound messages from the dolphins?

Experience the power of quantum transformation on all levels; health, relationships, career, and finances?

Clear past painful blocks and traumas in your life?

Discover and express your soul's divine purpose and personal mission to manifest your dreams and serve humanity at this critical time in humanity's evolution?

Rayna Lumbard, MA, LMFT
InnerSuccess Transformations
Mind/Body/Spirit Therapy and Healing
20688 Fourth Street, Suite 8
Saratoga, CA 95070
408-605-9195
Rayna@InnerSuccess.com
www.InnerSuccess.com

HAWAII IN AUGUST
BY KIM TOBIN

It was a very hot and humid afternoon during the last part of August here in eastern Missouri. It was the kind where all I wanted to do was go from an air-conditioned vehicle to an air-conditioned home. As I drove into the driveway, I could feel that something was off. Peanut, our light-brown and white paint horse was jogging from pasture to pasture. Peanut will not even jog to the barn for morning feeding. But, where was Stella? Stella is our rescue pony who just showed up in our pasture over eight years ago. Obviously, she's an escape artist!

I rushed to the pasture to see what Peanut was so upset about and there I found Stella, only she was on the other side of the fence in our neighbor's pasture with over fifteen other horses. This was not good. The closest gate was a two-mile walk from our house to the neighbors. That was not the biggest problem. The other horses were running Stella up and down the fencerow. Did I mention it was extremely hot? Stella also has a breathing problem. What on earth was I going to do? My mind raced trying to figure out how I was going to lead Stella across the neighbor's field to their gate with all those horses.

I ran to the fence to find the hole Stella escaped from and tried to guide her back into our pasture. However, the other horses had her so upset she could not calm down or slow down enough to come to me without another horse blocking her. By this time, I was panicking. How am I going to get those other horses away? The only thing that came to mind was to look up in the sky and say, "Hawaii, I'm going to need some help here."

Oh, Hawaii! My four-legged soulmate. We first set eyes on her in June of 2006. My husband and I already had Peanut and wanted a pasture buddy for her. We visited our local rescue ranch to see what was available. We went from stall to stall, talking and petting all the horses. Then, there was Hawaii. She was so tall and white with little brown freckles here and there. Hawaii was so tall! At six-foot-two, my husband could barely see over her back! I could almost see straight under her! She had the biggest, deepest brown eyes. We walked her out of the stall and into a small ring were we could get to know her better. She had a kind and gentle manner. I fell in love immediately.

We put in our papers to adopt Hawaii that day. Unfortunately, she could not come home with us until November. She had been rescued from such atrocious conditions, she still needed medicine and to be closely watched by the farrier. Actually, six months before they considered not rescuing her, as she was that close to dying. They grouped together and lifted her into the crowded trailer. I was beyond thankful they did not leave her.

How was I ever going to wait six months for her to come home? Even though the rescue ranch was more than ninety minutes away from our house, I went visit Hawaii on the weekends. We grew closer and closer with each visit.

Once November arrived, we were inseparable. We worked on trusting each other day in and day out. She finally came to know that she would always have food, water, shelter, and most importantly, love. I could do anything with that horse. I joke and say that we had such a bond I could walk between her back legs. I did not ever try, but knew I could.

Our bond continue to grow until a hot day in August when Hawaii got pneumonia. The vet estimated her age to be about thirty-five years old, which is pretty old for a mare that had been through hell before we got her. She was having trouble breathing and the vet said she was in pain. I already knew this. I had spent several nights in the barn with her. Hawaii had told me it was time for her to go. It was one of the hardest days of my life. Hawaii knew how much I loved her and I knew how much she loved me. I said my good byes, hugged her tightly, and went to my room and cried harder than I had in years. My husband held her while the vet put her to sleep. I just could not do it. I still hate August!

Here we are again in August and Stella is running out of breath. She's panicking too. "Hawaii, I'm going to need a little help here!" I could not believe my eyes as seven of the horses literally ran over the hill away from us! This calmed Stella and I a bit. However, the main two horses that were chasing Stella continued. I looked to the heavens again and said, "Hawaii, that was great, but damnit, I need more help!" A big wind came up, and the horses stopped in their tracks. In the very next instant every single horse ran full blast over the hill–every horse but Stella! She finally settled enough that I could show her how to get back in our pasture. "Thank you Hawaii! Thank you!"

I immediately fixed the fence and looked Stella over to make sure she was not hurt. She went to the water tank and drank just fine. **I went into the barn and cried tears of gratitude, while releasing the fears and loving the proof that Hawaii is still with me!**

I have had several strong bonds with horses and dogs over my lifetime. I am grateful beyond words for each one. I know for a fact that they never leave our side, even though they leave this Earth. Each of those animals that crossed my path and crossed the bridge to heaven bring me comfort, joy, and love every time I think of them.

Have you had a special bond with your furry family member? Have you talked to them since they passed? Have you seen, heard or felt them near you? I firmly believe that animals of all kinds are here to be in service to us, to help us on our path in this life. We just have to remember to ask for their help!

When working with furry family members and their humans, I often ask them for a list of things that remind them of their pets. I even ask this if the pet is still with them. Why is this important? This is one of the first ways animals start to communicate with their owners. For instance, does your cat have a pink collar with a bell? Has there been an instance where you needed to pick up medication or pet food for your fur-baby and the ring of a random bell reminded you to make the stop? That's the beginning of animal communication.

Let's say your furry family member has crossed the bridge and you hear a bell or see another pink collar. Did you instantly think if your baby?

Or, was there a time when you threw a bright green ball for your puppy to play fetch? When you see another bright green ball does that make you think of him? All of this is animal communication. It js their way of telling you that they are with you, and that they have something to say or to remind you to do.

Another process I ask my clients to work on is talking to their pets, even when they are away from them. I have often talked to my dogs when I am away at the office and there is a storm. My beagle hates storms. I talk to him to remind him that he is safe and that I will be home shortly. I have also asked that if he hears me to send me a sign, something only the two of us know about. Could be a butterfly, could be bird or a squirrel (Bubby loves chasing squirrels).

Whether I am working with a pet who has crossed over or is still with us, I try to remind the humans to ask for their animals' help. As you can see by my story, it never hurts. I firmly believe that animals come into our lives for many different reasons, but always in service to us. **Love and communication do not have to stop when they cross that rainbow bridge.**

Kim Tobin

Kim Tobin is a transformation mentor, business strategist, radio show host, author, and speaker helping spiritual women clearly acknowledge and embrace their unique gifts that fears often conceal. Kim is passionate about helping women align with their souls' gifts, enabling her clients to celebrate their divine inner magic and create the life they boldly desire. Kim works virtually with her clients from her office in Missouri, offering transformational programs and classes as well as in person at beautiful locations around the world. Learn more about Kim at **www. KimberlyTobin.com** and download her gift: "Through Fear to Fabulous– Learning to be You.

Twitter - @Clarity_Kim
Instagram - @magical.ceo
Facebook – Mystical.CEO

A FORCE OF NATURE
BY AERIOL ASCHER

It was a very difficult period of my life. I was extremely depressed after the loss of my dog Easter, who was in fact the third dog I had lost in just three-year period. Maxx was the first to go, on the day of my grandfather's birthday, and Ruby went just eighteen months later coincidently on my grandmother's birthday. My precious Easter went suddenly in my arms when his little body could no longer hold him there with me.

During this time the days were long and my heart was heavy, and it made it pretty difficult to do my work of being out in the world as a speaker and as a performer. I thank the universe for my clients because as I served them with energy healing, aromatherapy and vibrational sound, I was able to be in that sacred space of healing vibration myself. It was a plan so perfect and divine I never could have conceived I would be my primary client.

As an energy healer, I always recommend that my clients pay attention to the messages they get from spirits, or from their dreams or their subconscious.

So, when I had a "feeling" that I would add another dog to my collection, I was positive that it was simply not the case. My heart was definitely closed to that idea.

Our days went on. I liked our routine and I was still grieving. I was embracing my idea of whole self care and struggling still with some parts. Ziggy took on protecting his Grandma and had a permanent seat upon the throne of her cozy lap, while his older and wiser big sister Dali lay content next to her basket of balls nearby.

When I first started having dreams, I chose to ignore them.

I was really happy that I rescued Dali, whom Ziggy and I went on a big adventure road trip to bring home with us. But, sometimes I worried about Ziggy, as he had lost his Easter pal whom he tormented and loved.

It seemed that Ziggy was having the time of his life since he started therapy dog training courses and was quite a little celebrity at our local PetSmart. But Ziggy had nobody to play with.

The dreams and the feeling continued to get stronger and more frequent. It was just like voices in my head, and they often felt like small hunches.

In a dream one night I saw an actual picture of a small dog with a mask on its face. I also had a feeling that Easter somehow was leading me to this dog. I did not quite know what to make of this but I was sure I was not ready for another dog.

But sure enough, I had the dream again. I saw the face so clearly that I could not ignore it. I immediately went to the Humane Society website and looked at the rescue dogs on the website. I noticed a new dog featured as their dog of the week, perched like a little prairie dog. Oh, how lovely she was with her perky ears and masked face; she was such a sparkler! I was struck deeply by her little tongue peeking out as Easter's once did, and was hypnotized by that cute, masked face. If I was going to be in integrity with what I expected of my clients, I was going to have to follow these dreams encouraging me to keep my heart open to another dog.

I marched into our family room the following morning and announced to everyone that Easter had sent me a message that our next dog was at the Humane Society and I was going to go take a look.

I met our new little star just before Thanksgiving. They were calling her Savannah, and she rolled right over to show her little spotted pink belly to greet me. Oh, how her precious energy radiated through me; it really did touch my heart. I had to be smart, however and I made a date to bring Ziggy in the next day for a meet and greet. I am sure you can see how the rest of this part of the story goes. Little did we know that we had invited a force of nature into our home who was bound to be a shining star in our life.

Ziggy and our new edition got on well, although he was a little perturbed when his new baby required him to up his game in the training department. I had never in my lifetime thought that our mellow and easy-going Dali would be the one I had to worry about when we brought the new puppy home. Dali was quick to aggressively set boundaries, showing that she was the big mama and that Savannah, now re-named "Twinkie", was the new kid in town.

The influx of puppy love and the joy that Twinkie brought to the house was amazing. She breathed life into the home and caused my mother and I to combine forces in her training, because she was certainly a handful! She did all kinds of crazy things; she ran out the front door and in front of a school bus, took herself for a walk at the speed of light down the block, checked out the neighbor's yard from secret holes in the fence, tormented Ziggy, chased and barked at tons of squirrels, got sprayed by a skunk in the middle of the night, and pounced in my bed to tell me about it...the list goes on. She is a crazy little force of nature, and the spark of joy that kept us from letting the energy of our home. The joy this little sparkler brings is amazing.

I found her so amazing in fact that I had her DNA tested. I had done Dali's and luckily Easter's before he had passed away. Now I want you to take note here that I had always stated I did not want a Jack Russel Terrier because they were known to be too smart and stubborn, with abundant willpower and crazy energy.

I am sure you have figured out that Twinkie is part Jack Russel right? You got it. She is also part Chihuahua, which we suspected, and mini Italian greyhound. Had I known any of this I would have never invited such an adorable, clever, curious, and extremely fast and fearless creature into my life!

Twinkie has been through all of her training classes and is hopeful to do more tricks. She needs the classes to quiet her busy mind, although she is already doing everything Ziggy does and bossing him and Dali around all the time now. Talk about girl power! Twinkie is like part fairy and part ultra-empowered super boss girl. She totally keeps us on our toes. And what a star! The people over at the DNA website even featured her as the "Mystery Breed" of the month. I cannot imagine where being the honored mama of this super star will lead. I only hope I have the stamina to keep training her and Ziggy. They bring me so much joy.

My point in sharing this story is that I want the reader to take note that you can overcome your grief, even if it is buried deep. Just decide that it is time to let it go and be willing to forgive so that your heart can recover to its open and loving natural state. I want you to know that you can open your heart and love again. I want you to know that your emotional healing is importing, and that your connection with nature and with your own intuition is imperative to your healing, and to your humanity.

If you have suffered from severe trauma or grief, focus on your emotional and spiritual health by increasing your self-awareness, and remaining open to the possibility of healing. You are going to want to get yourself some support if you have had any major stress or emotional trauma.

Your emotions need to be released. The stuck emotions stay in your body. Allow the high frequency energy of joy and love to penetrate depression or any of the emotional barriers you have created in your energy or in your physical body. **I see our relationships with animals as such important parts of our lives.**

Here are my favorite ways to connect more deeply to your knowingness, and remedies for heart related emotional traumas, including grief, loss, depression, fear, anger and finding equilibrium, balance, and forgiveness.

1. **Connect deeply with nature**. Attune yourself to both the sounds and the silence of nature. Breath deeply and connect with your inner self. Let the sounds guide you inside and release trapped emotions both in the physical and emotional parts of ourselves. I often have my clients use crystals as part of this practice.

2. **Connect with animals.** Develop connections with animals to heighten empathy, build self-esteem, heighten awareness, etc. You may even think about getting an emotional support animal.

3. **Aromatherapy.** Another way I invite nature into my life to aid in emotional healing is through **aromatherapy.** I use aromatherapy in my practice assist clients to support and clear the emotional body. It is nature's little pick-me-up when it comes to emotional healing. Much more than just a wafting fragrance, these oils are made up of tiny plant molecules that absorb directly into the bloodstream for an instant emotional uplift.

4. **Learn and utilize energy healing.** I encourage you to master your own energy system and develop a daily practice. Use energy healing in addition to connecting with nature. I visualize these two working together, as nature brings the spark to the energy work, and I see this as how you acquire self- mastery.

5. **Trust your intuition.** Trust emotional information and the feelings that you get. This is your intuition telling you something. Try to notice what brings them up and if you let them flow. You will notice that your animal friends do not think twice about their senses. **Animals do not need to cover up their impulses or emotional states by trying to look good in the presence of others.**

A quick side note on touch: I have to say, Ziggy's warm belly next to me for a cuddle or Twinkie's endless kisses (although they are sometimes more up the nostrils than I care for) have given me unconditional loving support and pulled me out of many inner storm clouds I navigated during my times of grieving or depression.

The devoted companionship has been abundantly rewarding and the relationships I have developed with each of my fur babies has been far greater that the efforts and training classes we have put into them. I suppose that is how we must look at all of our earthly relationships.

In my chapter in *Experts and Influencers the Leadership Edition*, I spoke about my concept of whole self care. I see this as mind and body, as well as emotional and spatial care, that we must embrace for ourselves in a disciplined way to support our growing awareness and consciousness.

As previously stated, while you can do energy work and cultivate a daily practice, it is also important to seek a mentor or spiritual guide to assist you in your journey. Whole self care must include healing to address any pain in the physical body. Please also take great care to support yourself with emotional clearing and spiritual healing. Have a team of healing practitioners and call on them frequently to support you in your whole self care practice.

I know that after a loss or after trauma in one's life, it can seem like things will never return to normal again. I want you to know that this is only true if that is your choice. Allow yourself to feel your feelings deeply, and most of all allow yourself to let go of low frequency emotions like anger, blame, or judgement so that you can open yourself to the joy and love that will always exist in nature.

I hope that these words help support you and inspire you to take care of yourself, including welcoming into your life that animal connection that has been calling to your heart and spirit.

Aeriol Ascher

Aeriol Ascher, Author, Speaker, Teacher, Holistic Healing Master, Intuitive Guide and Voice & Presence Coach, has been in the field of self-care and personal development for 25+ years. Before closing its doors in 2017, her Holistic Healing Practice: Reiki Angel Intuitive Arts was voted Best Day Spa in Silicon Valley by the *San Jose Mercury News*, and her signature Reiki Angel Massage was voted best massage four times.

Aeriol empowers her clients with tools to increase body awareness, hone intuition, and connect to their highest selves so they can confidently show up, speak up, and stand out in their personal and professional lives. She has a passion for facilitating group healing experiences that awaken self-awareness, inspire growth, and create a safe and sacred learning environment for spiritual awakening, personal empowerment, and fun.

An advocate for self-expression and women in leadership, Aeriol loves to assist her clients to align with their most authentic selves so they can embody their most powerful presence and let their souls shine. Aeriol is available for speaking engagements, group and individual training, coaching, and private healing sessions, both live and via video conferencing technology.

Aeriol lives in San Jose, CA with her fur family consisting her dogs Ziggy, Twinkie, Dali, and their fifteen-year-old cat, Aengus. (Photo with rescue dog Dali).

More about Aeriol: **www.AeriolAscher.com**
Healing Practice: **www.SomaSoundTherapy.com**
Podcast: **www.HealingBodyMindandSoul.com**

Social Links:
www.facebook.com/askaeriol
www.facebook.com/somasoundtherapy
www.instagram.com/askaeriol/
www.twitter.com/askaeriol
www.youtube.com/user/ReikiAngelMassage
www.linkedin.com/in/aeriolascher/

A DREAM COME TRUE
BY MYRIAM PACHECO

I was a quiet, introverted, and lonesome child. Someone who when called upon by the teacher to answer a question was always unsure of herself, and someone who when teams were being picked was more than likely always picked last. I grew up and that shy little girl stayed with me; she was always in the back of my mind, always so unsure of herself. Needless to say, that little girl still resurfaces sometimes, not often, but she does make herself known.

That little girl wanted one thing in the world more than anything else: she wanted a puppy and that longing stayed with me as well. I would beg my parents over and over for a puppy, but there were always excuses, always "maybe-when-you're-older" empty promises, and when my sisters were born there were two extra voices added to the chorus of pleas. I think it took over ten years of pleas and hundreds of maybes for our little trio to wear my parents down enough for them to allow us to bring a pup into our home. That moment in time will be forever imprinted in my memory.

It was a late night in early March, my sisters and I had kicked our begging up a notch for the past few months, coming up with fantastical reasons as to why a dog would be the perfect addition to our family of five: *he'll be our brave protector...he'll make us go out on walks...he can eat the food I don't want...he will be like another baby for you mom!* Honestly, I think our incessant begging finally wore them down, and **that late March night they finally told us that we would begin looking for a pup to bring our family number to six.** I am not ashamed to admit that I burst out crying, and then outright sobbing, I was so very happy.

By this time I had been a vegan for a year and knew from the bottom of my heart that I wanted to adopt a shelter dog, and so the quest for the perfect dog for our family began. Now, my mom had some very clear specifications; she wanted a small, white dog, not too furry, and it had to be housetrained. I set out to find the dog that would make us all happy. It did not take too long for me to find a small rescue for Jack Rusell Terriers in San Francisco, CA. We began the adoption process, and first emailed the rescue and told them that we were very much inexperienced with dogs and that we really wanted a Jack Rusell Terrier. We got a quick response and they assured us that they would help us find the perfect dog for us. Meanwhile, we would spend afternoons discussing what his name would be, and everyone threw in a different name: *Oliver, Pluto, Koda,* etc. Out of all the names thrown out Cooper was the name that made us the happiest, and so Cooper it was.

We finally got word back from the rescue around the last week of March. They had a dog for us; he was a Jack Rusell-Maltese mix, and a young pup with a shy personality and some hang-ups about humans. Underneath those words was the first glimpse at him. **He was a scraggly little thing, with untamed white fur and big worried eyes. He was perfect.**

For the next week we prepared the house for his arrival, and then it was finally time to pick him up. As we drove up to San Francisco, my tummy fluttered with nervous excitement and my mind raced with wild thoughts of what he would be like. We met with the woman who was fostering Cooper, a kind, elderly biker who loved animals almost as much as her motorcycles, and then we finally got to see him.

There he was: a trembling little thing, he would not approach us and hid behind a chair, his whole being trembling from his ears to the tip of his tail. Finally, his caretaker picked him and handed him to my very reluctant and very surprised father, and to everyone's surprise Cooper seemed to calm down. He was handed to every member of the family and then he was handed over to me, and in that moment, I felt my heart melt. **He was everything my heart had longed for, and there he was in my arms. I did**

not want to let go of him, he was mine, my Cooper. All of the instructions given to me flew over my head, and all I could think about was the little dog in my arms.

The next few days with Cooper were a bit of a blur, but all I knew was that I had never been so happy in my life. There was a lot of trial and error with him, but he was a patient boy and took it all in stride. We soon learned that he was easily spooked, that he enjoyed chicken treats the most, and that he had loved playing tug of war with his toy bears. In a few weeks he had blossomed from a shy, introverted pup into a vivacious little boy full of energy. He still had some hang-ups about people, mostly adults, and would sometimes recede back into being an introverted little dog scared of the whole world. It took over a year for him to fully accept my dad, but since he accepted him they are the best of friends, always accompanying one another. **Since Cooper came into our lives he has proven himself to be one of the most amazing, most loving, most essential parts of our lives.**

Rescuing a dog is not something that people should overlook; rescuing quite literally saves the life of an animal who would have otherwise been euthanized for lack of room in shelters. When we began looking for a dog I demanded that he needed to be from a shelter or rescue organization in the Bay Area. According to the ASPCA, approximately 6.5 million companion animals enter shelters every year. Of those, around 3.3 million are dogs and 3.2 million are cats, and this is only in the United States. Imagine all of those animals, and now think about the fact that approximately 1.5 million companion animals are euthanized because there is not enough room in shelters. If more companion animals were adopted instead of bought there would be fewer animals that would have to go to shelters.

So how can we make this happen? We can encourage others who are looking for a new furry companion to look at their local shelters and rescues; now there are tons of ways to find your perfect furry companion online, with just a quick search and a few clicks. There are about 3.2 shelter animals that are adopted each year. We can also encourage others to donate their money or time to their local shelters and rescues, because a little help never hurt anybody. And lastly, we can also help by fostering. Fostering is a great way to help our local shelters and rescues, as it allows them to care for the animals better and takes some of the pressure of off their backs.

Having had Cooper in my life for the past two years, my life has changed a lot. I have become happier, and with my little furry pal by my side, I feel like I am never as lonely as I used to feel before him. He is a constant light whenever the world feels a little too dark, and in a way we have come out of our shell a little bit more together. That does not mean that we are the life of the party, but we can certainly hold our own now. I have honestly come to appreciate those quiet nights with Cooper nestled at my side as I work, or those mid-afternoon play sessions when he seems to truly let go and will just run and play fetch to his heart's content. In a lot of ways **Cooper and I have grown together;** I, from that little girl scared out of her mind, and him from that nervous wreck that sometimes hid under the bed. I can one hundred percent testify that having a companion dog in my life is the best decision I ever made, and I can testify that adopting him was the best choice for both him and my family. In him we found the sixth member of our family, that last missing piece that was just a little out of reach. **Cooper is my dream come true; he is all I ever longed for and more, and that little girl's dream has finally been fulfilled. All of the begging, pleading, and crying was worth having him in my life. He is worth all that and so much more.**

Myriam Pacheco

Myriam Pacheco was raised in the San Francisco Bay Area. She grew up with a love of the arts, literature, and nature. Myriam is a communication studies major looking to branch into the fashion and film industry, primarily as a journalist. Aside from her love of the arts, Myriam is an animal advocate who began her journey into a compassionate lifestyle from the time she was a young girl. She began by becoming a vegetarian when she was in high school and later on transitioning to a completely vegan lifestyle. Myriam lives her life day to day hoping to inspire others to follow through with adopting a compassionate lifestyle one day at a time.

Email: myriam.m.pacheco.s@gmail.com
LinkedIn: www.linkedin.com/in/myriam-pacheco
Twitter: @myriam_pacheco_
Instagram: @myriam.pacheco.s

Closing Thoughts...

I hope you have been touched by these beautiful, inspiring stories as much as we have enjoyed bringing them to you. I hope that the truth of the stories, profound lessons learned, and encouraging messages these authors have shared will empower you in your own life journey!

The publisher of this book, RHG Publishing™, is one of our family of organizations whose mission is to **help people live on purpose and with purpose in their lives and businesses.**

I invite you to read some of our other books, listed below, that are designed to share the passion, heart, and wisdom of Rebecca Hall Gruyter and a community of experts in many fields–all with the collective mission to equip and inspire YOU to create a purposeful life and to SHINE in your brilliance!

There are other ways to engage with us through: Your Purpose Driven Practice™, RHG TV Network™, and RHG Media Productions™. Please read on to find out more about what we offer to our community and all around the world.

We can't wait to see you, hear from you, and celebrate you as you share the gift of you with the world! May you always choose to **live on purpose and with great purpose...and SHINE!**

****

Other books compiled or written by Rebecca Hall Gruyter to be released in 2019 and 2020:

The Experts & Influencers Series: Women's Empowerment Edition

This powerful anthology will feature up to 30 experts and influencers committed to empowering you in the area of Women's Empowerment. They will share tips, advice, and powerful insights to help you step forward as a leader in your life and business. *(To be released June 2020)*.

Bloom and Shine!

This is a 365 Daily Inspiration anthology featuring up to 50 authors that provide daily inspiration for the reader to stop, pause, reflect, and be inspired and empowered by, in order to step into sharing the gift of who they are more fully in their life–one day and one step at a time. This book will then equip and empower the reader to live each day on purpose and with great purpose. The world needs more of you and your brilliance! *(To be released in October of 2020)*.

Step Into Your Mission and Purpose!

This anthology featuring up to 30 authors (the second book in the "Step Into" anthology series) will empower readers to discover and embrace their brilliance. This book will then equip and empower the reader to discover their mission and purpose, so that they can live each day on purpose and with great purpose. The world needs you and your brilliance! *(To be released in January of 2021)*.

Anthologies available now, compiled by Rebecca Hall Gruyter:

<u>"SHINE Trilogy Series"</u>
> **"Come out of Hiding and SHINE!"** (Book 1)
> **"Bloom Where You are Planted and SHINE!"** (Book 2)
> **"Step Forward and SHINE!"** (Book 3)

<u>"Step Into Series"</u>
> **"Step Into Your Brilliance!"** (Book 1)
> **"Step Into Your Mission and Purpose"** (Book 2 to be released in January 2021)

<u>"Experts & Influencers Series"</u>
> **"Experts & Influencers Series: Leadership"** (Book 1)
> **"Experts & Influencers Series: Women's Empowerment Edition"** (Book 2 to be released in June 2020)

<u>"The Grandmother Legacies"</u>
> <u>**"Empowering YOU, Transforming Lives"**</u> (365 Daily Inspiration Anthology)

Books available featuring chapters by Rebecca Hall Gruyter:

"**The 40/40 Rules**" Anthology compiled by Holly Porter

"**Becoming Outrageously Successful**" Anthology compiled by Dr. Anita Jackson

"**Catch Your Star**" Anthology published by THRIVE Publishing

"**Discover Your Destiny**" Anthology compiled by Denise Joy Thompson

"**I Am Beautiful**" Anthology compiled by Teresa Hawley-Howard

"**The Power of Our Voices, Sharing Our Story**" Anthology compiled by Teresa Hawley-Howard

"**Succeeding Against All Odds**" Anthology compiled by Sandra Yancey

"**Success Secrets for Today's Feminine Entrepreneurs**" Anthology compiled by Dr. Anita Jackson

"**Unstoppable Woman of Purpose**" Anthology and workbook compiled by Nella Chikwe

"**Women on a Mission**" Anthology compiled by Teresa Hawley-Howard

"**Women of Courage, Women of Destiny**" Anthology compiled by Dr. Anita Jackson

"**Women Warriors Who Make It Rock**" Anthology compiled by Nichole Peters

"**You Are Whole, Perfect, and Complete - Just As You Are**" Anthology compiled by Carol Plummer and Susan Driscoll

****

Dear Powerful Reader,

Do you want to reach more people? Do you wish to be part of inspiring and supporting others with your message, your gifts, and the work that you bring to the world?

Then I want to share some opportunities for you to consider.

The family or organizations that comprise Your Purpose-Driven Practice.com serves people like you globally in these powerful ways:

Each year we compile and produce anthology book projects, support authors in publishing their own powerful books as best sellers, produce and publish an international magazine, launch TV shows, facilitate women's empowerment conferences, increase people's visibility in major media, launch radio and podcast shows, help experts and speakers step into a place of powerful influence to make a global difference, provide programs and strategies to help you reach more people, and facilitate the Speaker Talent Search, which helps speakers, experts, and influencers connect with more speaking opportunities.

We would love to support you in your efforts to reach more people. Please take a moment to learn a little bit more about us at the sites listed below, and then reach out to us for a conversation. **We would love to help you be Seen, Heard, and SHINE!**

You can learn more about each of these things at our main website: **www.YourPurposeDrivenPractice.com**

Enjoy our powerful **TV and podcast shows: www.RHGTVNetwork.com**

Learn more about the **Speaker Talent Search™:**
www.SpeakerTalentSearch.com

Learn more about our **writing opportunities:**
http://yourpurposedrivenpractice.com/writing-opportunities/

If you would like to connect with me personally to explore some of our opportunities in upcoming book projects, podcast/radio shows, and/or TV, use this link to schedule a time to speak with me directly: **www.MeetWithRebecca.com**, or email me at: **Rebecca@ YourPuposeDrivenPractice.com**

May you always choose to Be Seen, Heard and SHINE!

Warmly,

Rebecca Hall Gruyter

Made in United States
North Haven, CT
20 July 2025

70861532R00078